VISUAL QUICKSTART GUIDE

ADOBE
AUDITION 1.5

FOR WINDOWS

Jeff Partyka

Peachpit Press

Visual QuickStart Guide
Adobe Audition 1.5 for Windows
Jeff Partyka

Peachpit Press

1249 Eighth Street
Berkeley, CA 94710
510/524-2178
800/283-9444
510/524-2221 (fax)

Find us on the World Wide Web at: www.peachpit.com
To report errors, please send a note to errata@peachpit.com

Peachpit Press is a division of Pearson Education

Editor: Stephen Nathans
Project Editor: Cliff Colby
Production Coordinator: Myrna Vladic
Copy Editor: Judy Ziajka
Compositors: Rick Gordon, Emerald Valley Graphics and Deborah Roberti, Espresso Graphics
Indexer: FireCrystal Communications
Cover design: The Visual Group
Cover production: George Mattingly / GMD

Notice of Rights

Notice of Liability

Trademarks

ISBN 0-321-24750-7

9 8 7 6 5 4 3 2 1

Printed and bound in the United States of America

Dedication

With love to Lauren Wiley–my wife, my best friend, and my best source of inspiration and encouragement. Thanks for steadying me as I navigated the sometimes treacherous terrain of authoring my first book. And also to our as-yet-unborn first child, whom we first learned about right in the middle of this project.

And also to my parents, Jeff and Beverly Partyka, who nurtured (and put up with!) my profound love of music for so many years.

Acknowledgments

I could not have written this book without the significant encouragement, ideas, and contributions of my editor, Stephen Nathans. His input strengthened this book considerably. He always responded to my questions, frustrations, and late-night phone calls with good humor and understanding. His flexibility and easygoing manner, even when the pressure was on for both of us, saved my sanity more than once.

I'm thankful to Judy Ziajka for going above and beyond the call of duty as a copy editor, helping to make these chapters much clearer and more readable than they were as first drafts. I also sincerely thank Cliff Colby at Peachpit for giving me the opportunity to realize my long-held ambition to write a book, and for being so helpful and responsive to my inquiries throughout the project.

TABLE OF CONTENTS

TABLE OF CONTENTS

INTRODUCTION

As a songwriter and musician who has been recording original music for more than 20 years, I've worked with a number of editing, mixing, and recording tools. Like many musicians, I also have a treasured collection of vinyl records, and I've spent countless hours carefully archiving my LPs to CD.

I've been excited to add Adobe Audition to my arsenal of audio tools. It has a remarkably rich palette of features and functions for studio musicians and hobbyists with a variety of musical ambitions. We'll explore many of those features and functions in this book.

If you're new to Audition, it may make sense to go through this book sequentially, chapter by chapter, and follow along as we introduce you to Audition's many cool features. If you've used Audition or its predecessor, Cool Edit Pro, you may use this book as more of a reference, zeroing in on chapters or sections that are particularly applicable to your current project or interest. Either way, I hope you find the book informative, clear, and useful.

What Is Audition?

Adobe Audition is an audio recording, editing, and mixing application for Windows 2000 and XP. It's loaded with features designed to appeal to a variety of audio and video professionals. Typical users include staff in recording and mastering studios, broadcast and post-production facilities, and video production houses.

Audition began its life as Cool Edit Pro, which Syntrillium Software unveiled in 1997 as a step up from its popular Cool Edit shareware program. Adobe Systems acquired the product in May 2003. The company renamed it Audition and added it to its suite of digital video tools for Windows, which also includes Premiere Pro, After Effects, and Encore DVD. In doing so, Adobe aims to provide video studios with a smoother workflow and an easier way to develop high-quality soundtracks for their projects.

You can import video files (AVI, WMV, MPEG, and others) into Audition and watch them while you record, replace, enhance, or tweak the corresponding audio. In addition, if you bring a WAV audio file into Adobe Premiere Pro or After Effects, you can use the Edit Original command to open the file in Audition and perform any of the wide variety of editing tasks the program offers.

With Audition, you can create, edit, loop, and add effects to individual sounds (including the more than 5,000 royalty-free loops included with the program); mix them together in a multitrack "recording" environment (using up to 128 tracks); and even prepare professional-quality masters. You can also choose between more than 50 digital signal processing (DSP) effects, filters, and restoration tools. You can use all your favorite third-party VST effects, too. ReWire support, new in version 1.5, allows you to stream high-resolution audio from other ReWire-enabled applications, including Propellerhead Reason and Ableton Live, directly into tracks in an Adobe Audition multitrack environment.

You can take advantage of 32-bit processing and sample rates up to 10 MHz. You can restore old recordings and improve their sound by manually or automatically removing clicks and pops from digital transfers of vinyl records and hiss from transfers of old tapes. Audition also lets you use equalization and effects to tweak the sound to suit your tastes and needs. You can mix and match disparate audio elements into one new composition, using volume, tempo, and key matching to blend them into a seamless whole.

What's New in Version 1.5?

Adobe didn't change much between Cool Edit Pro 2.5 (the latest revision when Adobe acquired the program) and Audition 1.0. But with the release of Audition 1.5, Adobe has introduced an impressive list of new features. They include the following:

◆ Improved support for video, including the ability to watch video frames in the Audition Timeline.

◆ Integrated, gap-free audio-CD burning for the creation of reference discs and replication-ready masters.

◆ New manual and automatic pitch-correction effects.

◆ Automatic click and pop removal for improved transfers from worn vinyl records and other flawed source material.

◆ The ability to reduce or even remove vocal or instrumental content with the Center Channel Extractor tool, which allows you to create *a cappella* music or vocal-less tracks for your next karaoke party.

◆ ReWire support for audio streaming to and from other ReWire-ready audio applications.

◆ Integrated support for third-party VST effects.

◆ Frequency space editing, which allows you to edit or add effects to frequency- or time-specific sounds as selected with a marquee selection tool.

◆ Clip time-stretching, for lengthening the duration of a sound file without changing its pitch.

◆ New sample sessions and hundreds of new royalty-free loops.

What's in This Book?

This book begins with two chapters on Audition and digital audio basics. You'll learn how to install Audition, configure it to suit your needs and your projects, and organize your files and scripts. These two chapters also introduce you to the fundamentals of digital audio, from sample rates and bit depths to MIDI.

Chapters 3-6 focus on the creation, capture, and manipulation of audio in preparation for larger projects. You'll learn how to record audio from external sources (including analog ones such as LPs and cassettes) and how to tweak it to make it sound the way you want. These chapters also cover the creation and management of audio files and introduces you to the basics of sound editing and the use of effects.

Chapters 7-10 walk you through Audition's multitrack capabilities. You'll learn how to loop sounds, import MIDI files, and mix disparate audio elements to create a satisfying and integrated whole. You'll also learn how Audition can help you create multichannel mixes of your work for use in high-resolution DVD projects, and you'll discover how Audition can help you create a professional-quality CD master.

The last two chapters cover some of the "extras" in Audition, including its ability to restore audio and work with video applications.

System Requirements

To use Audition and to perform the tasks in this book, your system should meet the following requirements:

◆ Microsoft Windows 2000, XP Home Edition, or XP Professional Edition

◆ Intel Pentium or AMD Athlon 400 MHz or faster processor (2 GHz or faster recommended)

◆ 64 MB of RAM (512 MB or more recommended)

◆ 75 MB of available hard-disk space (700 MB recommended for CD premastering)

◆ 800 × 600 color display (1024 × 768 display recommended)

◆ Stereo sound card (multitrack sound card recommended)

◆ CD-ROM drive

◆ CD-RW drive for recording audio CDs

◆ Microsoft DirectX 9.0 software for video import

◆ Speakers or headphones (recommended)

◆ Microphone (optional)

Additional requirements for use of Audition's multichannel encoder include the following:

◆ Windows XP for multichannel Windows Media Audio (WMA) import

◆ DirectX 8.0 and a multichannel sound card and DirectSound driver

ADOBE AUDITION BASICS

In this chapter, we'll get to know the basic components of the Audition interface: the windows and views that you'll need to start navigating as soon as you've installed the program and opened it for the first time. I'll introduce you to the three main *views*, or environments, in Audition—the Edit, Multitrack, and CD Project views—all of which you'll learn about in more depth as you proceed through this book.

Audition offers more buttons, commands, menus, and features than one chapter can possibly cover, so I'll focus only on the absolute basics here. Rest assured that I'll get to the other important functions in subsequent chapters. Now let's get started!

Installing Adobe Audition

If you've ever installed a program on a PC, you'll find the Audition 1.5 installation process to be straightforward. Before you get started, make sure that your computer system meets the minimum requirements (see the introduction to this book), and that you have your product serial number handy.

To install Adobe Audition:

1. Insert the Audition CD into your computer's CD-ROM drive. The setup program should begin automatically; if it doesn't, browse to the setup.exe file on the CD and double-click it.

2. After the introductory screen, the setup program asks you to select a language. Choose one. Your choices are English, French, German, and Japanese (**Figure 1.1**).

3. Read and accept the end-user license agreement.

4. On the next screen, enter a name, organization, and serial number (**Figure 1.2**); then click Next.

   You'll find the 24-digit serial number on a sticker on the back of the Audition jewel case.

5. Select a destination on your computer's hard drive for the Audition program files (**Figure 1.3**); then click Next.

   A default location will be offered, typically in the Program Files folder, which guarantees that Audition will be accessible from the Start menu. You may also specify your own choice by typing it or browsing to an alternative location.

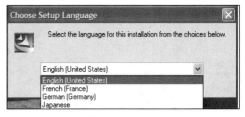

Figure 1.1 The installer's language menu.

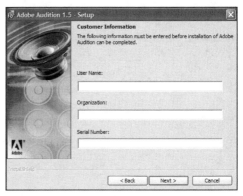

Figure 1.2 You'll be asked to enter a user name, organization, and serial number during the installation.

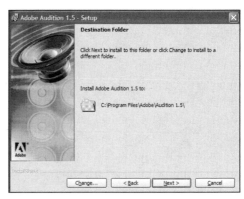

Figure 1.3 You can accept the installer's default destination folder for the Audition application files, or click Change to make your own choice.

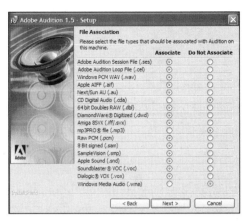

Figure 1.4 The File Association window.

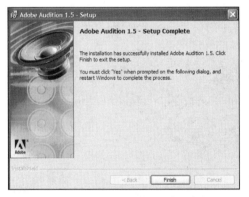

Figure 1.5 You'll be asked to click Finish and then restart your computer at the end of the setup process.

6. In the next window, you'll see the default file associations the setup process will create for Audition (**Figure 1.4**). Any file of a type associated with Audition will open in Audition by default once the installation is complete. Accept the default settings, or make changes as you see fit. Then click Next.

7. You'll see a window indicating that the setup program is ready to install Audition. Click the Install button, and the process will begin. When it's complete, the setup process will finish (**Figure 1.5**), and you'll be prompted to restart your computer.

The Audition Windows

When you first open Audition, you'll see a menu, a toolbar, a status bar, and a series of windows. We'll be discussing the various commands and options in the menus and toolbars throughout the book, but let's take a quick look now at the windows (**Figure 1.6**).

THE AUDITION WINDOWS

Organizer window   *Display window*

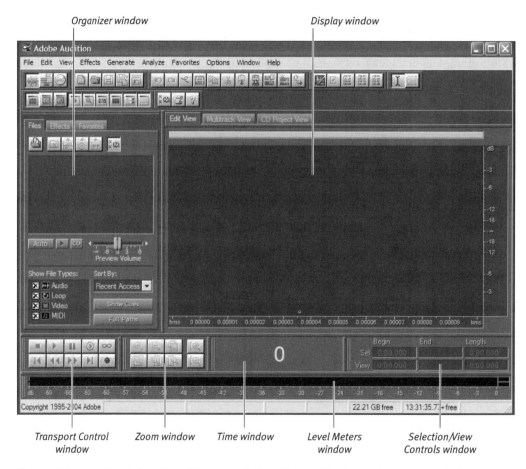

*Transport Control   Zoom window   Time window   Level Meters   Selection/View
window   window   Controls window*

Figure 1.6 These are the windows that will be present in the Edit view of the Audition interface by default when you open the program for the first time.

◆ The **Display window** is by default the largest component of the Audition interface. It shows the currently open waveform, multitrack session, or CD playlist, depending on which view you're in. For more on views, see "Selecting a View" later in this chapter.

◆ The **Organizer window** displays a list of your open files and gives you easy access to various effects, including your Favorites list. It's located to the left of the Display window by default, but you can drag it to other locations. You can even move it so it's separate from the interface, floating in its own separate window, although you'll find that it's much easier to keep the elements of your project distinct when windows are nested or docked.

◆ The **Transport Control window** provides 10 controls for your file or session: Stop, Play, Pause, Play from Cursor to End of File, Play Looped, Record, Go to Beginning or Previous Cue, Rewind, Fast-Forward, and Go to End or Next Cue.

◆ The **Zoom window** provides eight buttons for controlling the view in the Display window: Zoom In Horizontally, Zoom Out Horizontally, Zoom Out Fully Both Axes, Zoom In Vertically, Zoom Out Vertically, Zoom to Selection, Zoom In to Left Edge of Selection, and Zoom In to Right Edge of Selection.

◆ The **Time window** monitors the time elapsed during recording or playback. By default, the time display format is *mm:ss:ddd* (*minutes:seconds:milliseconds*), but you can change the setting by right-clicking the window and selecting an alternative.

continues on next page

THE AUDITION WINDOWS

◆ The **Selection/View Controls window** shows where in time the visible waveform or session (or a selected clip within, if you've made one) begins and ends, as well as its total length. The display format conforms to the setting currently selected in the Time window.

◆ The **Level Meters window**, located by default at the very bottom of the Audition interface, allows you to monitor the level of incoming and outgoing audio signals. On the right side are the red clip indicators; these light up to warn you if either level exceeds 0 db.

By default, all of these windows are docked in the interface. You can undock or reposition any of them, except for the Display window. The dockable windows have a pair of lines running along a side or along the top (**Figure 1.7**). When you roll the mouse over the lines, a special cursor appears, and you can grab the window and drag it to the center of your work area until you see a separate outline. The window is now separated from the interface, floating above it. You can position it wherever you like on the screen. Alternatively, you can drag your window to another dockable location.

Dockable-window lines

Figure 1.7 This pair of lines in a window indicates that the window is dockable.

✔ Tip

■ To prevent a floating window from redocking as you move it, hold down the Ctrl key as you drag.

The Status Bar

At the very bottom of the Audition interface, you'll see the status bar (**Figure 1.8**). You can customize it to display the information you want simply by right-clicking it and using the pop-up menu (which is also accessible from the View menu at the top of the screen). You can also use the menu to toggle between showing and hiding the status bar.

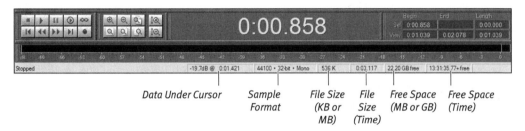

Data Under Cursor   Sample Format   File Size (KB or MB)   File Size (Time)   Free Space (MB or GB)   Free Space (Time)

Figure 1.8 The Audition status bar.

Status Bar Content

You can display the following information in the status bar:

◆ **Data Under Cursor** displays precise information—stereo channel, amplitude, time—about the audio indicated by your cursor in the Display window.

◆ **Sample Format** displays the current sample and bit rate of an open file.

◆ **File Size** shows the size of your file in kilobytes or megabytes.

◆ **File Size (Time)** shows the length of the audio measured in time.

◆ **Free Space** shows the amount of hard disk space left on your computer. (When you're creating a playlist in preparation for burning a CD, it can display the amount of time left on a 74-minute or 80-minute disc.)

◆ **Free Space (Time)** indicates how much recording time you have left based on the current sample rate and your hard disk space.

◆ **Keyboard Modifiers** shows whether the Ctrl, Alt, or Shift key is currently pressed.

◆ **SMPTE Slave Stability** shows how stable an SMPTE (Society of Motion Picture and Television Engineers) timecode is, indicating how well the timecode is synching with Audition's internal clock. (See Chapter 12 for more on SMPTE.)

Selecting a View

Audition offers three main views, each with its own unique functionality: Edit view, Multitrack view, and CD Project view.

All three views share important features and components. They all offer the convenience of menus and toolbars and windows that allow you easy access to Audition's range of features.

To toggle the views:

◆ *Do one of the following:*

▲ Click one of the view tabs at the top of the Display window (**Figure 1.9**).

▲ Open the View menu and select the view you want to use.

▲ Use the 8, 9, and 0 number keys on your keyboard. Pressing 8 opens Edit view, 9 opens Multitrack view, and 0 opens CD Project view.

▲ Click one of the view buttons on the left side of the toolbar atop the main window (**Figure 1.10**).

✔ Tip

■ If you prefer not to use the tabs at the top of the Display window, you can hide them by going to the View menu and unchecking Show View Tabs.

Figure 1.9 The view selection tabs at the top of the Display window.

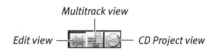

Figure 1.10 The view selection buttons.

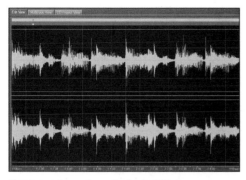

Figure 1.11 A waveform display in Edit view.

Figure 1.12 A spectral display in Edit view.

Edit View

You use Edit view to open, edit, and save changes to individual sound files. You can view your files using Waveform view, which is the default selection, or Spectral view.

Waveform view presents a visual representation of the audio signal, displaying a series of positive and negative peaks based on the amplitude of the sounds in relation to time (**Figure 1.11**). The horizontal x axis measures time, while the vertical y axis measures amplitude. With a stereo file such as the one in Figure 1.11, the window is split into two separate images: one for each stereo channel (with the left one on top).

In Spectral view, the y axis displays changes in frequency rather than amplitude (**Figure 1.12**). Spectral view allows you to determine the prevalence of specific frequencies in an audio clip. You can still find amplitude information as well; it's represented by the range of colors, with dark blues signifying low amplitudes, and bright yellows indicating high ones.

Toggling between the Waveform and Spectral views:

- ◆ *Do one of the following:*
  - ▲ From the View menu, select Waveform view or Spectral view (**Figure 1.13**).
  - ▲ Click the Waveform/Spectral view toggle button on the toolbar (**Figure 1.14**).
  - ▲ Press the F9 key on your keyboard.

✔ Tip

- ■ When you make changes in Edit view and then save your file, the file is permanently changed to reflect your changes. This is called *destructive* editing. One of the ways that Multitrack view differs from Edit view is that it offers *nondestructive* editing: the changes are not saved to your individual sound files.

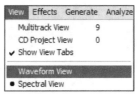

Figure 1.13 You can use the View menu to switch between Waveform and Spectral views.

Figure 1.14 You can use this button to toggle between Waveform and Spectral views.

Multitrack View

Multitrack view (**Figure 1.15**) is the view you use to combine individual sounds to create a multilayered composition. It functions very much like a traditional multitrack tape recorder, complete with panning and level adjustments and the ability to add effects.

Any changes or edits you make to your composition in Multitrack view are nondestructive: the individual sound files themselves are not altered as you work. This increases the drain on your computer's processor, but it facilitates on-the-fly tweaking of your sounds. You can change your settings and hear the results immediately during playback.

When you create a multitrack composition and want to save your work, Audition saves it in a *session file* (with the .ses file extension). Session files record information about the sound files you're using and all of your mix settings. They are usually small files because the real meat of your mix—the individual sound files—is saved separately and only needs to be referenced.

✔ Tip

■ It's best to save session files in a dedicated folder along with your original sound files, particularly if you're in the habit of moving sessions among various computers. Keeping everything in one place makes migrating to other machines much easier.

Figure 1.15 In Multitrack view, you can assemble your multilayered composition.

MULTITRACK VIEW

CD Project View

In Audition 1.0 and Cool Edit Pro, you needed to render your project to a WAV file and run a CD recording program like Easy CD Creator or Nero to burn it to CD. The CD Project view (**Figure 1.16**), new in Audition 1.5, eliminates the need for a separate CD-burning application. Here, you can assemble tracks for and burn CDs directly from Audition itself.

The Display window in CD Project view contains the playlist, from which you can manipulate properties of individual tracks, including artist and title tags, copy-protection settings, and the gaps you want (if any) between tracks.

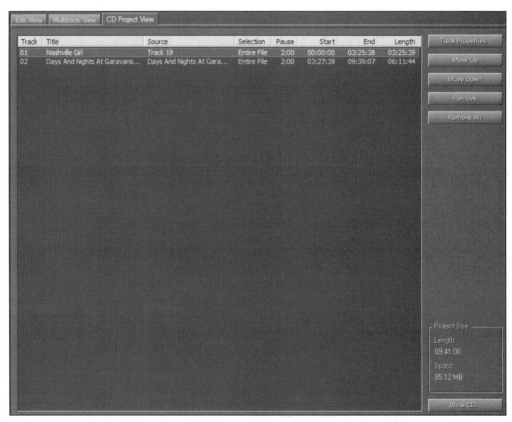

Figure 1.16 CD Project view lets you burn a CD of your Audition project directly from the program.

INTRODUCTION TO DIGITAL AUDIO

2

Digital audio teems with terms and concepts that might seem intimidating to someone who's never worked with it. It's a complex topic, and while it isn't necessary to become an expert in it to use tools like Audition and get great results, you'll need to become familiar with some basics so that you can manipulate digital audio intelligently.

In this chapter, I'll introduce some of the terms and concepts you should understand as you begin to use Audition—waveforms, analog and digital audio, sampling rate, bit depth, dithering, and MIDI—which will be relevant as you move forward through this book and into your work with Audition.

Waveforms

If you've ever worked with digital audio on a computer, you're probably familiar with waveforms (**Figure 2.1**). A waveform is a visual representation of an audio signal, showing changes in amplitude (vertical *y*-axis) over time (horizontal *x*-axis). The peaks and valleys in a waveform represent positive and negative pressure. If you zoom in while looking at a waveform in Audition, you'll find that you can see (and edit and tweak) the individual peaks and valleys quite readily (**Figure 2.2**). (I'll get into the editing and tweaking in Chapter 5.)

When working with stereo audio, you'll see two waveforms in Audition. The one at the top represents the left channel, and the one at the bottom represents the right channel (**Figure 2.3**). You can work with both channels at once or with one at a time. The latter approach can be handy if the two stereo channels are out of phase with each other. When this happens, a signal peak in one channel's waveform corresponds to a valley in the other, which can lead to a weakening, or even the disappearance, of the signal. You can use the Invert effect in Audition to address this situation (see Chapter 6).

Figure 2.1 A waveform is a visual representation of an audio signal.

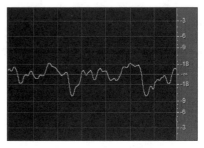

Figure 2.2 Zooming in on a waveform in Audition can give you access to tiny snippets of audio.

Left channel

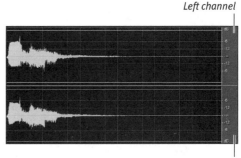

Right channel

Figure 2.3 The top half of a stereo waveform shows the left channel, and the bottom half shows the right channel.

Analog and Digital Audio

As its name suggests, recorded analog sound is analogous to the original sound wave that created it. Look closely at the grooves of a vinyl record containing music with a sudden, loud crescendo (many classical records are good examples). You should be able to see quite clearly where the crescendo is on the record; the width of the grooves changes along with the amplitude of the sound. (Analog tape works similarly, except that it's the magnetic particles on the tape—rather than grooves—that record, reflect, and reproduce the changes in sound.)

Digital audio is quite different. In digital recording, an analog-to-digital converter (ADC) captures samples of the original sound at a steady rate. The ADC converts the captured samples into a specific series of numbers, or bits, which make up the digital-audio file stored on a computer or compact disc. The term *bit depth* refers to the number of bits that are used for each sample. More bits per sample means wider dynamic range, less extraneous noise, and more accurate sound reproduction.

To be played, digital audio must be converted to analog format, since that's what headphones and loudspeakers can reproduce. That's why CD players and computer sound cards contain digital-to-analog converters (DACs).

Sampling Rate and Bit Depth

The higher the sampling rate of a digital file (measured in samples per second), the more frequencies that file can reproduce. Frequency refers to the number of sound waves or "cycles" repeated per second, measured in hertz (Hz). A 10 kHz frequency, for example, is a sound containing 10,000 cycles per second. The frequency of a sound determines its pitch; low frequencies produce low-pitch sounds, and high frequencies produce high-pitch sounds. The human ear can hear frequencies ranging from 20 Hz to about 20 kHz.

According to Nyquist's theorem, which says you have to be able to take two complete samples per second to reconstruct an accurate waveform, for a particular frequency to be captured in a digital file, the sampling rate must be at least double that frequency's value. So a recording containing a peak frequency of 12,000 Hz, for example, would require a sampling rate of 24,000 samples per second.

A file's bit depth affects the range of amplitude, or volume, that the file can capture. A file with a larger bit depth will have more dynamic range than one with a smaller bit depth. When audio is captured in a digital format, each sample is assigned the most appropriate amplitude value among those available.

With a 16-bit depth (the standard for audio compact discs), 65,536 amplitude values are available. In contrast, millions of amplitude values are available with higher bit depths such as 24- and 32-bit (which is the highest bit depth that Audition supports). For this reason, I recommend that you do your digital audio recording and editing at the highest bit depth possible, even you have to downsample the resulting file to a lower bit depth later in the editing process.

Dithering

Downsampling audio to a lower bit depth—for example, from 24-bit to 16-bit for CD mastering—can result in harmonic distortion due to bit truncation. You'll most likely hear the effects of this in quiet segments of your audio; they might sound broken up or otherwise distorted. To compensate for the ill effects of bit truncation, you can use dithering.

When you use dithering, you're actually adding a small amount of random, low-level noise to your audio. The purpose of this noise is to make the transitions between truncated bits less audible and to cover up the distortion created during downsampling.

Dithering Options

When you choose the Edit > Convert Sample Type option in Audition and choose a lower bit depth, Audition gives you several dithering options (**Figure 2.4**). Experiment with these settings when converting to lower bit depths to see which give the best results for the audio you're working with.

◆ **Dither Depth (Bits):** Allows you to choose how much dithering to apply to your signal. Values between 0.2 and 0.7 are usually optimal; they provide the benefits of dithering with the least amount of residual noise.

◆ **p.d.f.:** Stands for probability distribution function. This setting offers five methods for introducing dithered noise into your audio: Rectangular, Triangular, Gaussian, Shaped Triangular, and Shaped Gaussian. Triangular is usually recommended as the most workable combination of noise modulation, distortion, and decreased signal-to-noise ratio.

◆ **Noise Shaping:** Allows you to assign different noise levels to different frequencies. Your choice among the various noise-shaping curves will depend on the content of your audio and your sample-rate and bit-depth settings.

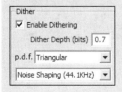

Figure 2.4 You can configure dithering options in Audition's Convert Sample Type window.

Data-Handling Options

Before you get started using Audition, you should choose Options > Settings and check the Data tab (**Figure 2.5**). It contains a number of settings for you to configure:

◆ **Embed Project Link Data for Edit Original Functionality:** Select this option to create links between sessions (used in multitrack recording in Audition) and mixdown files (used in Adobe Premiere Pro and After Effects). If you enable this setting, you can open Audition and tweak your multitrack audio files from within a mixdown file that's open in Premiere Pro or After Effects.

◆ **Auto-Convert All Data to 32-Bit Upon Opening:** Select this option to convert all audio opened in Audition to 32-bit automatically, no matter what the original bit rate. This option can be attractive because edits made in 32-bit mode generally result in better-sounding audio than those made in lower bit depths.

◆ **Interpret 32-bit PCM .wav Files as 16.8 Float:** Select this option to ensure compatibility with 32-bit PCM WAV files created in older versions of Audition or Cool Edit.

◆ **Dither Transform Results (Increases Dynamic Range):** Select this option to enable dithering when applying certain effects (see Chapter 6 for an overview of effects available in Audition).

◆ **Use Symmetric Dithering:** Select this option to prevent the dithering process from introducing DC bias, or offset, to your waveform (see Chapter 3 for information about DC bias).

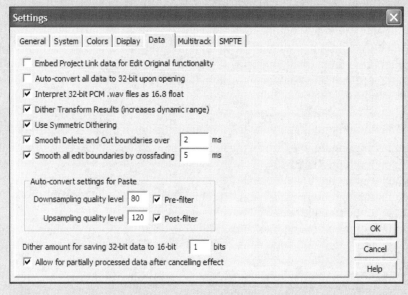

Figure 2.5 Choose Options > Settings and click the Data tab to configure various data-handling options.

continues on next page

DITHERING

Data-Handling Options *(continued)*

◆ **Smooth Delete and Cut Boundaries over *n* ms:** Select this option to help prevent audible clicks at splice points in a waveform, such as at places where you've cut or removed audio clips.

◆ **Smooth All Edit Boundaries by Crossfading *n* ms:** Select this option to use crossfades to prevent audible clicks or other jarring transitions at edit points in a waveform. Crossfading refers to the overlapping of the end of one piece of audio and the beginning of another (think of the way radio stations avoid gaps between songs by starting one song a few seconds before another ends). Enter a value in milliseconds to specify the length of the crossfade.

◆ **Auto-Convert Settings for Paste:** Configure these settings to specify how Audition should handle sample conversions for audio pasted into a waveform (audio will be converted to conform to the sample and bit rates of the waveform into which it's being pasted).

◆ **Dither Amount for Saving 32-Bit Data to 16-Bit:** Enter 1 in this field to enable dithering when pasting 32-bit audio into a 16-bit waveform. Enter 0 to disable dithering.

◆ **Allow for Partially Processed Data After Cancelling Effect:** If this option is selected and you click Cancel while Audition is in the middle of applying an effect to an audio selection, the effect will still be applied to the audio that was processed before you canceled the operation. In the same situation, if this option is not selected, the effect will be removed from all of the audio.

DITHERING

MIDI

Unlike digital audio files, Musical Instrument Digital Interface (MIDI) files do not directly reproduce sound. Rather, they tell MIDI-capable musical instruments and other devices how to reproduce music.

MIDI is a standard that was developed to allow sequencers and computers to communicate with musical instruments such as synthesizers via a particular type of cable (known, appropriately enough, as a MIDI cable). MIDI files can contain information about the musical notes and chords, sounds and synth voices, panning, and volume needed to reproduce a piece of music. When used in a computer program like Audition, this information is sent to a MIDI-capable sound card, which contains a mini-synthesizer that can play the music embedded in the MIDI clip. So one MIDI file can result in very different sounds, depending on the type and quality of the sound card used.

One of the main advantages of MIDI files is that they don't take up much space. A minute of MIDI music often takes up kilobytes rather than megabytes (as is common with actual digital audio files).

You can't use Audition to record MIDI files; the program supports only playback of MIDI files in multitrack compositions. Such files can be imported into a multitrack session as a clip; then you must assign them to a MIDI-capable output device so that they can be reproduced.

Figure 2.6 The MIDI Out tab of the Options > Device Properties window.

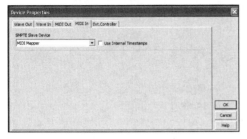

Figure 2.7 The MIDI In tab of the Options > Device Properties window.

✔ Tips

- You can specify the device you want to use for MIDI playback by choosing Options > Device Properties and opening the MIDI Out tab (**Figure 2.6**).

- On the MIDI In (**Figure 2.7**) and MIDI Out tabs that you open by choosing Options > Device Properties, you can configure Audition to use your available MIDI ports to send and receive SMPTE (Society of Motion Picture and Television Engineers) timecode. This procedure allows you to synchronize Audition with other MIDI applications or hardware.

MIDI

Audio Recording Today

Multitrack recording has been a fixture of professional audio recording for more than half a century. Pioneered by guitarist Les Paul, multitrack tape recording allows you to record multiple times on the same piece of tape without erasing what you recorded previously. For example, you can make a recording of a singer singing harmony with herself or of a guitarist overdubbing several parts.

With the advent of multitracking, groups of musicians no longer had to play live in the studio, which meant that they could combine and refine individual parts without having to stitch together perfect ensemble takes to make a record. In the 1960s, bands like the Beach Boys and the Beatles became known for using overdubbing techniques to record parts one at a time, doubling vocal and instrumental parts to create interesting and unusual textures.

For a long time, only professional recording artists had access to state-of-the-art sound in studios with top-quality multitrack recording equipment. By the 1980s, however, the growing availability of "portastudios" from TASCAM and others allowed more and more hobbyists, amateur musicians, and pros who wanted to do serious home recording to bring functional (if relatively crude) multitrack recording capabilities into their basement, bedroom, and garage studios.

Home-studio setups have now become more sophisticated thanks to the development of high-quality and affordable hardware and software, including Audition. Today, with the right equipment, aspiring musicians who have never seen the inside of a "real" studio can create professional-sounding recordings in their own homes.

MIDI

RECORDING SOUND

Before you can bring all of Audition's features to bear on your audio, you need to bring your audio clips into the program. And you need to configure Audition to work with the audio devices that are part of your computer system.

In this chapter, I'll detail the procedures for configuring Audition to work with your sound cards to record and play audio. I'll also show you how you can bring audio from disparate sources into Audition's Edit and Multitrack views for editing, saving, and composing.

Setting Device Order

Before you get rolling with Audition, you need to make sure you've configured it to use the proper devices in your system for recording and playing audio. This is particularly important if your system contains more than one sound card, for example, or MIDI devices.

The first thing you need to do when configuring Audition to play and record audio files is to select and sequence the audio devices on your computer that you want Audition to use. You use the Device Order window, accessed through the Options menu.

The Device Order window contains four tabs. Start by setting the Playback Devices tab and Recording Devices tab. You may want to use the same devices for both recording and playback, or you may have separate devices for each function.

To set playback device order:

1. In the Audition menu, choose Options > Device Order (**Figure 3.1**).

   The Device Order window opens.

2. Select the Playback Devices tab (**Figure 3.2**).

   The Unused Playback Devices pane of the tab lists the devices available on your computer that are capable of playing back audio.

3. Select the device that you want to use for playback in Edit view.

4. Click the Use in EV (Edit view) button.

   The [EV] marker will appear next to the device's name.

5. Select the first device that you plan to use for playback in Multitrack view.

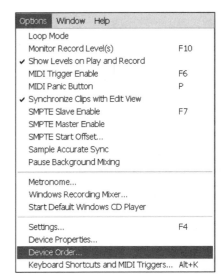

Figure 3.1 To choose and prioritize playback and recording devices for use in Audition, open the Device Order window, accessed via the Options menu.

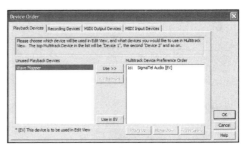

Figure 3.2 The Playback Devices tab in the Device Order window is where you specify the devices Audition should use for playback in the Edit and Multitrack views.

SETTING DEVICE ORDER

Figure 3.3 Use the Recording Devices tab to specify devices for recording audio; click Use to activate a device.

6. Click Use to move it to the Multitrack Device Preference Order pane.

7. If you want to move a device from the Multitrack Device Preference Order list back to the Unused Record Devices list, highlight the device and click Remove.

8. Repeat with any additional devices in the order you want to use them.

   You'll be able to assign different devices to different tracks in Multitrack view, but not until you've configured this setting.

To set recording device order:

1. In the Device Order window, select the Recording Devices tab (**Figure 3.3**).

   The Unused Record Devices pane of the tab lists the devices available on your computer that are capable of recording audio. You're configuring the preferred devices for recording incoming audio.

2. Select the device that you want to use for recording in Edit view.

3. Click the Use in EV (Edit view) button.

   The [EV] marker will appear next to the device's name.

4. Select the first device that you plan to use for recording in Multitrack view.

5. Click Use to move it to the Multitrack Device Preference Order window.

6. If you want to move a device from the Multitrack Device Preference Order list back to the Unused Record Devices list, highlight the device and click Remove.

7. Repeat with any additional devices in the order you want to use them.

continues on next page

✔ Tip

■ The MIDI Output Devices (**Figure 3.4**) and MIDI Input Devices tabs work similarly. You need concern yourself with these only if your system includes MIDI devices. See "Importing MIDI files" in Chapter 8.

Figure 3.4 The Device Order window also includes tabs for setting MIDI recording and playback devices.

Setting Up Devices: Don't Wait

The last thing you want to worry about in the middle of a complex multitrack Audition project is hardware configuration. It's best to set up everything properly from the start, so that Audition knows exactly what recording and playback devices are available, and which ones you want to use for which tasks.

If you fail to configure these settings properly, you'll have irritating problems down the road. You may hear nothing when you try to play audio in the Edit View. You may not be able to monitor incoming audio as it's being recorded. You may not be able to hear the MIDI files that you've imported in a multi-track session.

Instead of solving these problems one by one as they occur, spend a little time setting up your recording and playback device properties when you first open Audition. You'll be glad you did.

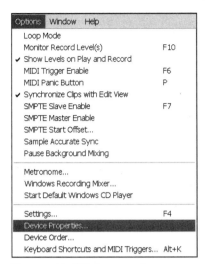

Figure 3.5 You'll find more settings to configure in the Device Properties window, accessible via the Options menu.

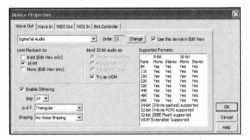

Figure 3.6 You can configure your playback device on the Wave Out tab of the Device Properties window.

Setting Device Properties

Another key step in configuring Audition to play and record audio is setting device properties. Among other things, you need to configure Audition's settings so that the application can deliver audio that your playback devices can reproduce, and you need to specify how the program should handle 32-bit audio, if you intend to use it.

To set device properties:

1. Choose Options > Device Properties (**Figure 3.5**).

2. Click the Wave Out tab and select a device from the drop-down menu. You can review its capabilities in the Supported Formats pane (**Figure 3.6**).

3. *Set any of the following:*

   ▲ **Order:** This field indicates the order number assigned to the device for use in the Multitrack view. You may have already configured this in the Options > Device Order window. If not, or if you want to change the setting, click the Change button to open the Device Order window and make the adjustment.

   ▲ **Use This Device in Edit View:** When this box is checked, Audition uses this device for audio playback in Edit view.

   ▲ **Limit Playback To:** If your sound card is capable of playing back only 8- or 16-bit files, but you're working with 32-bit audio, you can check one of these boxes to downsample the audio during playback. You can also set the device to play in mono in Edit view.

continues on next page

▲ **Send 32-Bit Audio As:** As long as nothing is selected in the Limit Playback To area, you can choose a setting here to specify how the software sends 32-bit audio to your device. Choose 3-byte packed PCM, 4-byte PCM, or 4-byte IEEE float.

▲ **Enable Dithering:** When this option is selected, Audition dithers audio from a file that's encoded at a bit depth higher than your sound device can support. Otherwise, Audition truncates the audio data, removing and discarding unused bits. (For more on dithering, see Chapter 2.)

4. Click the Wave In tab (**Figure 3.7**) and select the device you'll be using for recording audio. You can review its capabilities in the Supported Formats pane.

5. *Set any of the following:*

▲ **Get 32-Bit Audio Using:** This setting is analogous to the Send 32-Bit Audio As setting on the Wave Out tab. Here, you're specifying how you want your device to deliver 32-bit audio to Audition. The same options are available: 3-byte packed PCM, 4-byte PCM, and 4-byte IEEE float.

▲ **Multitrack Latency:** You need to set this field only if your device introduces latency to the recording process. Latency produced by a device usually results in one recorded track being out of sync with the others. Enter a value in milliseconds to compensate for a latency issue.

▲ **Adjust to Zero-DC When Recording:** Check this box if you need to remove DC bias during recording.

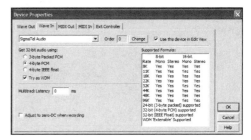

Figure 3.7 The Wave In tab of the Device Properties window.

SETTING DEVICE PROPERTIES

What is zero DC bias?

Due to flaws in recording devices or other hardware in a signal chain, audio waveforms can sometimes look askew in Audition's Edit view. In such cases, you may notice that the waveform isn't centered properly on the center line of the waveform graph (**Figure 3.8**). This is known as DC bias, or offset, and is caused by DC voltage from a faulty hardware device contaminating an audio signal.

The Adjust to Zero DC Bias checkbox compensates for hardware problems that lead to off-center waveforms, resulting in ones that are properly centered with zero DC bias (**Figure 3.9**). It's best to avoid off-center waveforms because they can sound noisier and murkier than centered waveforms, and the perceived amplitude is often reduced.

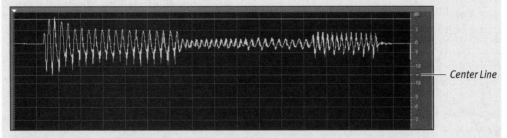
Center Line

Figure 3.8 In this case of DC bias, the waveform is off-center.

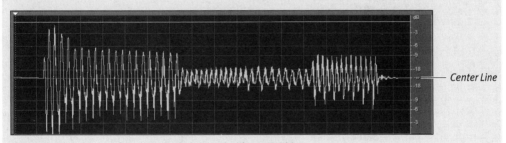
Center Line

Figure 3.9 Here the waveform is properly centered with zero DC bias.

SETTING DEVICE PROPERTIES

To configure Audition for use with an external controller:

1. In the Device Properties window, select the External Controllers tab (**Figure 3.10**).

   This tab enables you to configure Audition to work with an external controller such as the Mackie Control Universal. Such a controller allows you to bypass your mouse and keyboard and edit audio using "real" faders and controls.

2. Select a controller in the drop-down menu.

3. Select a volume increment setting.

4. Click the Configure button (**Figure 3.11**) to activate options offered by the software provided with your controller. Set the options.

✔ Tip

■ If you're using MIDI devices, you can make simple configurations in the MIDI In and MIDI Out tabs (see Chapter 2).

Figure 3.10 You can configure Audition to use an external controller.

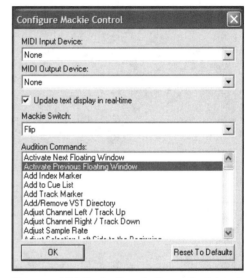

Figure 3.11 Click the Configure button on the External Controllers tab of the Device Properties window to manipulate the features available for your controller.

The Mackie Universal External Controller

Perhaps you're a veteran of all-analog recording and you miss the tactile feel of knobs and faders. Perhaps you just want an easier way to manipulate digital audio than a mouse and keyboard can offer. In any case, an external controller might be a worthwhile addition to your toolkit if you find the limitations of PC input devices unbearable.

The $1,299 Mackie Control Universal looks and feels like a conventional mixing board, with knobs, motorized faders, and panning pots. It's compatible not only with Adobe Audition but also with products such as Digidesign Pro Tools, Steinberg Cubase SX, Cakewalk SONAR 2.2, Mark of the Unicorn (MOTU) Digital Performer, and many others. For more information on Mackie Control products, visit www.mackie.com.

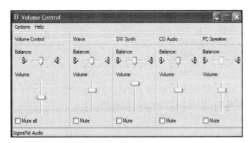

Figure 3.12 The Windows Volume Control window as it appears in Windows XP Home Edition.

Figure 3.13 The Properties window for the volume control allows you to adjust settings for your sound card.

Figure 3.14 Use these faders to control the level of incoming audio.

Recording Audio

Digitizing and storing audio is one of the core capabilities of Audition. You can connect microphones, musical instruments, tape decks, turntables, and just about anything else capable of transferring music to the Line In jack of your sound card for recording in Audition. You can record in either Edit or Multitrack view, and you can specify sampling rate, bit depth, and resolution to suit your equipment and the way you want your audio output to sound.

Audition also offers Timed-Record mode, which allows you to specify a maximum time for recording or to set Audition to record and stop recording at a particular time, as with a VCR.

It's a good idea to check the level of the source signal coming from your sound card before you start recording. You want to get a good, loud, "hot" signal—but not too hot, or your recorded audio will be marred by ugly digital distortion, known as clipping.

✔ Tip

■ The loudest part of your signal should peak somewhere between –2 db and 0 db in the Level Meters window.

To adjust your sound card's input level:

1. Locate and open the Windows Volume Control window (**Figure 3.12**).

   On my computer, running Windows XP Home Edition, it's located in Start > All Programs > Accessories > Entertainment.

2. Choose Options > Properties.

3. Select the Recording radio button and click OK (**Figure 3.13**).

   The Recording Control window opens (**Figure 3.14**).

continues on next page

4. Set the recording level with the faders that appear in the window.

✔ Tip

■ For a shortcut to the Recording window of the Windows mixer from Audition, choose Options > Windows Recording Mixer (**Figure 3.15**).

To record audio in Edit view:

1. *Do one of the following:*

▲ To create a new, blank audio file, from the Audition menu, choose File > New, or click the Create New File button on the toolbar (**Figure 3.16**).

▲ To record in an existing file, open the file and place the current-time indicator in the spot where you want your new recording to begin (**Figure 3.17**).

The current-time indicator is a yellow arrow and line that act as a cursor in the Display window. You place the current-time indicator by either clicking a spot in the waveform or dragging the yellow arrow to the right place.

2. Click the Record button in the Transport Control window to start recording.

3. When you're done, click the Stop button to stop recording (**Figure 3.18**).

✔ Tip

■ If you're worried about pressing the Record button accidentally, you can disable it by right-clicking it and selecting Disable Record Button (**Figure 3.19**).

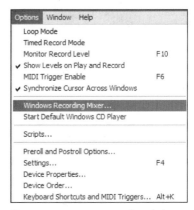

Figure 3.15 You can access the Windows Recording Mixer easily from Audition's Options menu.

 Figure 3.16 The Create New File button.

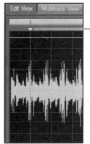

Current-time indicator

Figure 3.17 The current-time indicator is an arrow at the top of the Display window connected to a line that acts as a cursor in a waveform (Edit view) or multitrack composition (Multitrack view).

Stop   Play

Record

Figure 3.18 The recording and playback buttons at the bottom left of the screen.

Figure 3.19 To disable the Record button, just right-click it and select Disable Record Button.

RECORDING AUDIO

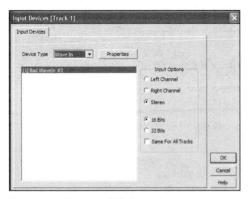

Figure 3.20 When you click the In 1 button next to a track in Multitrack view, you can select and configure the device from which you want to record.

To record audio in Multitrack view:

1. For each track to which you'll be recording, click the In 1 button in the Display window.

   Audition selects the correct sound card input (**Figure 3.20**).

2. Click OK.

3. Click the red Record-Enable button, marked R (**Figure 3.21**) for each track to which you'll be recording.

4. Make sure the current-time indicator is at the right place in the Display window, or make a selection to mark the desired place for your recording in the session.

5. Click the Record button to start recording.

6. Click the Stop button to stop recording.

✔ Tip

■ You can record on just one track or several at once.

Record buttons —

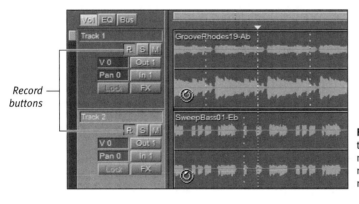

Figure 3.21 The R buttons for tracks 1 and 2 are both enabled, meaning that audio will be recorded on both tracks when recording starts.

To record audio using Timed Record mode:

1. Enable Timed Record mode *by doing one of the following:*

   ▲ Choose Options > Timed Record Mode.

   ▲ Right-click the Record button and select Timed Record Mode (**Figure 3.22**).

2. Click the Record button.

3. In the Maximum Recording Time field of the Timed Record Mode window (**Figure 3.23**), click the Recording Length button and fill in the desired maximum time.

✔ Tip

■ You can choose to start recording immediately by clicking the Right Away button in the Start Recording area, or you can set Audition, as you would a VCR, to start and stop recording at a specific time; click the At button and fill in the appropriate fields.

Figure 3.22 You can right-click the Record button and select Timed Record Mode to specify a particular length for a recording or to set a date and time for recording to begin and end.

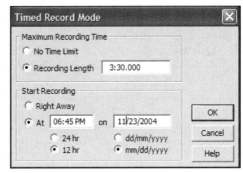

Figure 3.23 The Timed Record Mode window.

Figure 3.24 You can use File › Open to extract a track from an audio CD.

Figure 3.25 Navigate to your CD-ROM (or CD-RW or DVD) drive in the Look In drop-down menu and select the tracks you want to extract in the window below.

Extracting Audio from CDs

One way to bring audio into Audition is to import it from your existing CD collection. You can either digitally extract, or *rip*, audio directly from a CD, or you can record the audio within Audition itself.

Whenever possible, you should rip rather than record from a CD. Ripping uses digital-to-digital data transfer and thus guarantees higher audio quality and fidelity.

Also keep in mind that not all drives or drive configurations support analog audio recording (which is essentially what you're doing if you record from within Audition). If you have an internal drive, you must have the Audio Out cable connected to the drive to support analog recording. If your source drive is external, analog recording is not an option. But that's no big deal, because, again, ripping works better, and the process is much faster.

Audition provides two ways to rip audio from a CD. You can use the File > Open command for a quick and easy rip, or you can use the File > Extract Audio from CD option if you want more control over the process.

To extract CD tracks using the Open command:

1. Insert your CD into your PC's CD-ROM drive.

2. Choose Edit view and select File > Open (**Figure 3.24**).

3. Select CD Digital Audio (*.cda) as the file type to display and browse to the CD-ROM drive (**Figure 3.25**).

4. Select the tracks you want to extract and click the Open button.

   The track is extracted.

EXTRACTING AUDIO FROM CDS

To extract CD tracks using the Extract Audio from CD command:

1. Insert your CD into your PC's CD-ROM drive.

2. In either Edit view or CD Project view, choose File > Extract Audio from CD (**Figure 3.26**).

   The Extract Audio from CD window (**Figure 3.27**) appears.

3. In the Device drop-down menu, select the CD-ROM drive containing your CD.

4. In the Source Selection area, select either Track or Time.

   Select Track if you want to select one or more complete audio tracks to extract. Select Time if you want to select part of a track or a large block of audio that spans more than one track.

   The Time option can be handy when you're dealing with live CDs or when you want to extract more than one track to a single audio file.

5. Select a setting in the Interface Options area.

   In most cases, you'll want to use the ASPI/SPTI setting. Adobe recommends that the Generic Win32 setting (which uses input/output control codes instead of SCSI commands) be used only when the ASPI/SPTI setting causes a problem.

6. Select an Error Correction setting if appropriate.

   If your CD-ROM drive has built-in error correction, only the CDDA Accurate setting will be available. Otherwise, you will be able to change the setting to No Correction or Jitter Correction. Most modern drives perform well with the CDDA Accurate setting.

7. Click OK to extract the track.

Figure 3.26 For more advanced configuration options, use the File > Extract Audio from CD method.

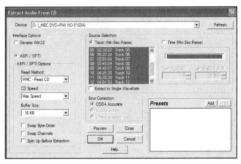

Figure 3.27 The Extract Audio from CD window.

✔ Tip

- If your computer has multiple CD-ROM drives, CD burners, DVD-ROM drives, or DVD burners, you can use any one of them to play CDs and as a source drive for ripping CD-Audio tracks. In general, drives that are CD-only (ROM or recorder) will rip faster and more reliably.

MANAGING AUDIO FILES

Given the nature of computer hard disk space (finite) and of audio files (large), you can't afford to be disorganized or a pack rat when working in Audition. It's important to know what files Audition is generating, where they reside on your hard drive, and how much space they're taking up.

In this chapter, I'll explain the Files tab in the Organizer window and how it can help you work with your files in Audition. I'll also discuss the methods for saving files and the file formats you can choose. Finally, I'll describe how, why, and where Audition creates temporary files as you work and what you can do to manage them.

Using the Files Tab

In Edit, Multitrack, and CD Project views, you can use the Organizer window's Files tab to easily manage your files (**Figure 4.1**). The Files tab lists all open audio, MIDI, and video files. From there, you can choose to edit your files, bring them into an open Multitrack session or CD playlist, or close them. You activate these tasks using the buttons at the top of the Files tab.

◆ The **Import File** button enables you to browse to and open the audio, MIDI, and video files you want to use.

◆ The **Close File** button closes the files currently selected on the Files tab list.

◆ The **Insert into Multitrack** button moves the selected files to a session in the Multitrack view. If you insert more than one file, Audition inserts each one into its own track.

◆ The **Insert into CD Project** button moves the selected files to a playlist in the CD Project view.

◆ The **Edit File** button moves the selected file to the Edit view for editing.

◆ The **Advanced Options** button toggles between hiding and showing the advanced options at the bottom of the Organizer window. These include options for choosing the file types displayed in the list, whether to show full paths for your files, and settings for previewing your files.

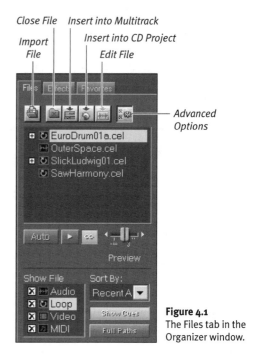

Close File Insert into Multitrack
Import File Insert into CD Project
Edit File
Advanced Options

Figure 4.1
The Files tab in the Organizer window.

USING THE FILES TAB

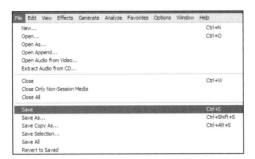

Figure 4.2 Choose File > Save to save an open file in Edit view.

Figure 4.3 The Save buttons on the toolbar.

Figure 4.4 Click the Options button in the Save As dialog box to configure settings particular to the file format you've selected.

Working with Audio File Types

Audition allows you to work with a range of audio file types. The types of files you use will depend on a number of factors: how much hard disk space you have available, what type of audio source you used to import your files, and what other programs you'll be working with. (For a complete list of supported file types, see the sidebar "Supported Audio File Types" later in this chapter.)

Audition offers a great deal of flexibility in audio file conversion. Once you've opened and edited a file in Audition, you can save it in the format that best suits your needs.

To save changes to a file currently open in Edit view:

◆ *Do one of the following:*
   ▲ Choose File > Save (Ctrl+S) (**Figure 4.2**) or
   ▲ Click the Save Waveform button on the toolbar (**Figure 4.3**).

   Audition saves the current file to the current location.

To save your changed file in a new format or as a separate file:

◆ *Do one of the following:*
   ▲ Choose File > Save As (Ctrl+Shift+S)
   ▲ Click the Save Waveform As button on the toolbar (Figure 4.3).

◆ In the Save As dialog box, browse to the folder in which you want to save the file.

◆ If desired, edit the name in the File Name field, and choose a file format in the Save As Type drop-down menu.

◆ Click Save.

   Audition saves the file in the chosen format or with the new file name to the selected location (**Figure 4.4**).

To save an identical copy of the file currently open in Edit view, leaving the original active and intact:

◆ *Do one of the following:*

▲ Select File > Save a Copy

▲ Click Ctrl+Alt+S.

◆ In the Save Copy As dialog box, browse to the folder in which you want to save the file.

◆ If desired, edit the name in the File Name field, and choose a file format in the Save As Type drop-down menu.

◆ Click Save.

Audition saves the file copy to the selected location.

To save just a portion of an open audio file as a new file:

1. In Edit view select the part you want to save.

2. *Do one of the following:*

▲ Choose File > Save Selection

▲ Click the Save Highlighted Selection button on the toolbar.

3. In the Save Selection dialog box, browse to the folder in which you want to save the file.

◆ If desired, edit the name in the File Name field, and choose a file format in the Save As Type drop-down menu.

◆ Click Save.

✔ Tips

■ To save all open files, choose File > Save All. If the files already exist on your computer, they will be updated to reflect any changes you've made. If one or more of them do not yet exist on your computer, a Save As dialog box will appear asking you to specify a folder location, a name, and a file type.

■ In the Save As dialog box, you can select the Save Extra Non-Audio Information check box to save information such as header and cue-mark data along with the file you are saving (See Figure 4.4). Beware of using such files in CD-recording applications other than Audition, however; some may convert the non-audio information to a burst of unpleasant extraneous noise added to the beginning of your track on the burned CD.

WORKING WITH AUDIO FILE TYPES

Supported Audio File Types

Audition can open and save your audio files in any of the formats in the following list. Depending on the one you choose, you may be able to configure various options by clicking the Options button in the Save As dialog box (**Figure 4.5**); for a comprehensive discussion of these options, see the Audition help files.

- Windows PCM (.wav)
- PCM Raw Data (.pcm or .raw)
- Windows Media Audio (.wma)
- 64-Bit Double (.dbl)
- 8-Bit Signed (.sam)
- A/mu-Law Wave (.wav)
- ACM Waveform (.wav)
- Amiga IFF-8SVX (.iff or .svx)
- Apple AIFF (.aif or .snd)
- ASCII Text Data (.txt)

- Audition Loop (.cel)
- Creative Sound Blaster (.voc)
- Dialogic ADPCM (.vox)
- DiamondWare Digitized (.dwd)
- DVI/IMA ADPCM (.wav)
- Microsoft ADPCM (.wav)
- MP3/mp3 Pro (.mp3)
- NeXT/Sun (.au or .snd)
- SampleVision (.smp)

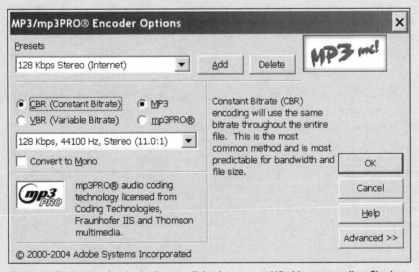

Figure 4.5 The Options box in the Save As dialog lets you set MP3 bit rates to adjust file sizes.

Choosing an Audio File Type

In general, when you want to save your work in an uncompressed format, it makes sense to use the Microsoft PCM, or WAV, file format. It can store mono or stereo audio at various resolutions, sample rates, and bit depths. Stereo 44.1 kHz/16-bit WAV files are typically burned to CD-Rs to make audio CDs; this is the standard for the uncompressed LPCM (linear pulse code modulation) format used in the Red Book specification for audio CDs. The 80-minute CD-Rs in common use today can accommodate 700 MB of such files. LPCM WAV files can get quite large (about 9 MB per minute of audio), so make sure you have enough disk space available if you plan to store a lot of them.

The common practice of streaming audio, or making it available for download, over the Internet has necessitated the availability of compressed audio-file formats, and MP3 and Windows Media Audio (WMA) are among the most popular. Audition supports direct encoding of both MP3 and WMA files with a variety of options; you'll want to consider using these if your audio will end up on the Internet or if file storage space is an issue.

If your source files are MP3 or WMA, don't bother re-encoding them as CD-quality WAV files if you don't have to. While MP3 and WMA use sophisticated algorithms to compress audio data, and sacrifice quality in some cases, you can't *add* quality by bumping the file up to WAV. The software doesn't restore any information lost in the compression process; it basically just blows some air into the file.

The Audition Loop (.cel) file format is similar to MP3, but it's optimized for use in looping applications. Typically, very short silences are added to an MP3 file during encoding, either at the beginning or end (or both). This would wreak havoc in a looping situation, so built into the .cel format is a header that stores information about these silences so that they can be removed when the file is looped.

Most of the other formats you can use when saving files in Audition are specific to particular platforms or applications, and you need only consider them when your project requires it. For example, if you typically transfer your work between Windows and Macintosh systems, you may find the use of the Apple AIFF format (an uncompressed format analogous to WAV in Windows) very handy; otherwise, you probably won't need to use it. If you're working primarily in Windows and Audition, WAV (uncompressed) or MP3 and WMA (compressed) files should cover you well in most situations.

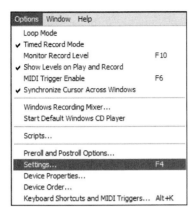

Figure 4.6 Choose Options > Settings to specify a folder to house your temporary (.tmp) files.

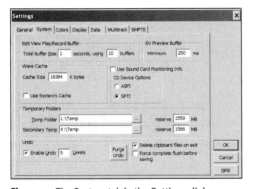

Figure 4.7 The System tab in the Settings dialog.

Figure 4.8 You can accept the default folder in the Temporary Folders field or specify your own choice.

Using Temporary Files

Whenever you work with audio files, you almost always make changes to them. Trimming, fading, normalizing, overdubbing, adding effects—all change the audio file that's open in Audition.

To facilitate and speed up editing (and to help make your edits reversible), Audition creates a temporary copy of the file during the editing process. The names of these temporary files begin with CEP, and they have the .tmp file extension.

None of us has infinite hard-disk space, and temporary Audition files can be surprisingly large. So you should check to see where Audition is keeping your temporary files, particularly if your computer has a partitioned hard drive (in that case, you should make sure the folder resides on the drive with the most available disk space and/or the highest speed).

To specify folders for storing temporary files:

1. Choose Options > Settings (F4) (**Figure 4.6**).

2. In the Settings window that opens (**Figure 4.7**), click the System tab.

3. In the Temporary Folders area, note the default Temp folder that Audition has chosen for you, or specify a different folder in the Temp Folder field (**Figure 4.8**). Make sure the selected Temp folder is on a drive with plenty of free disk space.

4. In the Reserve field, accept the default or specify a different value (in megabytes).

   This value sets the amount of space in the Temp folder; set a value high enough so that you don't run out of space in the folder.

continues on next page

USING TEMPORARY FILES

5. Click OK.

Audition applies the new values and returns you to the Edit or Multitrack view.

✔ Tip

- Specify a high Reserve value for your Temp folder if you plan to work with large numbers of files at once (say, in a multitrack session). In a case like that, determine the amount of free disk space available, and choose the highest Reserve value that seems feasible.

- Optionally, you can specify a second temporary storage folder in the Secondary Temp field. If you have a large amount of free space on the hard drive that houses your main Temp folder, it's usually not necessary to specify a second one.

Manually Deleting Temporary Files

Unless Audition is running, your temporary file folders should be empty. Audition automatically deletes all temporary files when you close a session. However, if either Audition or your computer crashes and therefore fails to close properly, unwanted (and often large) temporary files may be left behind.

If Audition is not running, you can simply browse to the Temp folder in Windows and delete the files. You can also get rid of existing temporary files from within Audition itself.

USING TEMPORARY FILES

Figure 4.9 To clear your temporary files while Audition is running, choose File > Manage Temporary Folder Reserve Space.

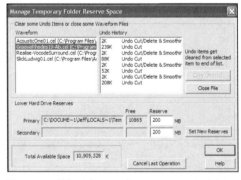

Figure 4.10 Select the waveforms you want to delete and click Close File.

To delete temporary files within Audition:

1. Choose File > Manage Temporary Folder Reserve Space (**Figure 4.9**).

2. In the window that appears (**Figure 4.10**), select the file in the Waveform list that you want to close.

3. Click Close File.

   Audition deletes the temporary file.

✔ Tips

■ You can also remove Undo tasks that have accumulated for a file. When you select a file in the Waveform list, a list of Undo tasks appears in the window next to it. You can select any Undo task and click Clear Undo(s).

■ You can change your reserve settings in the Manage Temporary Folder Reserve Space window by setting a new value in megabytes and clicking Set New Reserves.

■ Normally, Audition creates a temporary file only when you've edited a file. To force the program to create a temporary file at any time (if, for example, you're especially concerned that the complex edit you just made be recorded somewhere immediately, but you're not ready to save the file), choose File > Flush Virtual File.

USING TEMPORARY FILES

EDITING SOUND

Once you have an audio file open in Audition's Edit view, you'll likely want to edit it to suit your needs. The possibilities are numerous. You may want to trim silence from the beginning or end (or even the middle) of your file, or you may want to adjust the sample or bit rate. You may want to cut or copy clips for use in other Audition files or even in other audio or video applications. Audition makes editing your audio files easy.

In this chapter, I'll discuss the various ways you can view, mark, and select the audio you want to edit. I'll cover the selection techniques Audition offers, as well as the zooming, marking, and snapping tools that are available. I'll also describe techniques for cutting, copying, pasting, and deleting audio and for inserting or removing silence from a waveform. And I'll explain how to use Audition to change a file's sample or bit rate and convert a waveform from mono to stereo (and vice versa).

This chapter also serves as an introduction to Audition's audio restoration capabilities, which I'll discuss in more depth in Chapter 11.

Selecting Audio

Before you edit an audio file, you need to select a portion of the audio file that you want to cut, copy, fade, process, reverse, or otherwise alter. If you want to make a change to an entire file or multitrack session, you can press Ctrl+A, or choose Edit > Select Entire Wave (in Edit view) or Edit > Select All Tracks (in Multitrack or CD Project view).

Once you've made your selection, you may need to fine-tune its duration.

To make a selection in an open file:

1. Find the point in the timeline where you want your selection to begin or end.

2. Click directly on the waveform at the desired beginning or end point.

3. Drag the length of the desired section to make your selection (**Figure 5.1**).

   By default, the selection appears in white in the Display window.

✔ Tip

■ You can use a different color for selections by choosing Options > Settings, selecting the Colors tab, clicking Selection Highlight, and choosing a color (**Figure 5.2**).

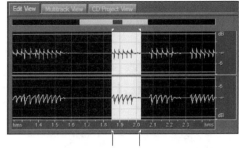

Selection start point   Selection end point

Figure 5.1 To make a selection in an audio file, just click the waveform and drag across the audio you want to select.

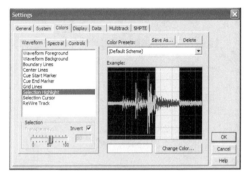

Figure 5.2 You can change the color used for selections on the Colors tab, under Options > Settings.

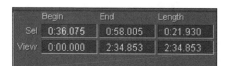

Figure 5.3 To fine-tune your selection to the thousandth of a second, use the timecode controls just below the Display window, at the far right of the screen.

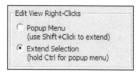

Figure 5.4 To enable selection extension via right-clicking, use the General tab under Options › Settings.

To shorten or lengthen your selection:

◆ *Do one of the following:*

▲ Hold down the Shift key, click the waveform, and drag the start point or end point to the desired new position in the timeline. (If you click the waveform without holding down Shift, the selection will become unselected.)

▲ Enter the beginning and end points in the timecode panel just below the Display window at the far right of the screen (**Figure 5.3**). Your start and end points will be adjusted in accordance with the timecode changes you enter.

✔ Tip

■ You can also extend your selection by right-clicking and dragging, but first you must choose Options > Settings, select the General tab, and select the Extend Selection radio button in the Edit View Right-Clicks field (**Figure 5.4**).

SELECTING AUDIO

49

To make a selection in the right or left channel of a stereo waveform:

1. Select the left or right channel *by doing one of the following:*

   ▲ Hover the pointer over the upper portion of the top half of the waveform (for the left channel) or the lower portion of the bottom half (for the right). A small L or R box will appear next to your cursor, depending on whether you're hovering in the left or right channel (**Figure 5.5**). Click once to place your cursor in the channel; double-click to select the entire channel.

   ▲ Click the appropriate button on the toolbar (**Figure 5.6**).

   ▲ Choose Edit > Edit Channel and select the channel (or channels) to edit (**Figure 5.7**).

   Audition will highlight the selected channel and dim the other one.

2. Make your selection from the waveform as described earlier in the task "To make a selection in an open file."

   The selection will be confined to the appropriate stereo channel.

✔ Tip

■ When you want to select the entire range of a waveform currently visible in the Edit view's Display window, simply double-click in the center of the window.

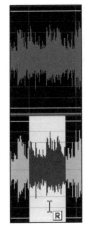

Figure 5.5 One way to make a selection in only one channel of a waveform is to hover the mouse over that channel until an "R" or "L" appears.

Edit Right Channel

Edit Both Channels

Edit Left Channel

Figure 5.6 On the waveform selection toolbar, you can choose to make your selection in one channel or both.

Figure 5.7 You can choose Edit > Edit Channel to specify whether you want to work with just the left or right channel of a stereo waveform, or both.

Time Selection tool

Marquee Selection tool

Figure 5.8 The Marquee Selection tool on the toolbar enables selection of particular audio frequencies in Spectral view.

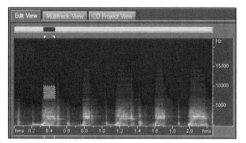

Figure 5.9 Once you've made a selection in Spectral view, you can fine-tune it by dragging or resizing.

Selecting Frequencies in Spectral View

You can use Spectral view within Edit view to select and edit particular frequencies. (For an introduction to Spectral view, see Chapter 1.) Selecting frequencies can be especially handy in restoration work; if you're working on a file with distortion that's limited to the higher frequencies, for example, you can select just those frequencies in Spectral view and edit them, leaving the other frequencies unchanged.

To select frequencies in Spectral view:

◆ Click the Marquee Selection tool on the toolbar (**Figure 5.8**) and drag across the desired frequencies in the Display window.

 Once you've made your selection (**Figure 5.9**), you can drag it to move it, or click an edge or corner to fine-tune its size.

✔ Tips

■ Use the Time Selection tool to make selections in Spectral view that cover all frequencies.

■ If you want to edit the frequencies in only one channel of a stereo file when using the Marquee Selection tool in Spectral view, use the Edit > Edit Channel menu to select the appropriate channel.

■ If the Time and Marquee Selection tools are not visible in the toolbar, choose View > Toolbars > Spectral Selection to activate them.

Selecting Using Zero Crossing Points

A zero crossing point is a point in an audio file where the amplitude is zero. These are usually good places to make edits because the chance of an audible artifact (a clicking or popping noise, for example) resulting from any edit you make is greatly reduced. When you've made a selection in Edit view, you can have Audition fine-tune your selection so that it begins or ends at the nearest zero-crossing point by using the Edit > Zero Crossings menu (**Figure 5.10**).

◆ **Adjust Selection Inward:** Locates and shrinks your selection to begin and end at the most convenient zero crossing points within your selection; this can also be accomplished by clicking the Zero Crossings button on the toolbar (**Figure 5.11**).

◆ **Adjust Selection Outward:** Locates and extends your selection at both ends to the nearest zero crossing points outside your selection.

◆ **Adjust Left Side to Left:** Extends the left edge of your selection leftward to the next zero crossing point.

◆ **Adjust Left Side to Right:** Extends the left edge of your selection rightward to the next zero crossing point.

◆ **Adjust Right Side to Left:** Extends the right edge of your selection leftward to the next zero crossing point.

◆ **Adjust Right Side to Right:** Extends the right edge of your selection rightward to the next zero crossing point.

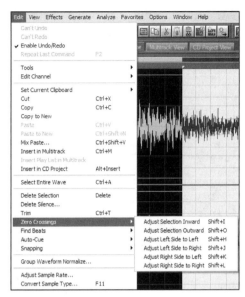

Figure 5.10 Use the Edit > Zero Crossings menu to extend your selection to the nearest zero crossing points.

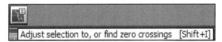

Figure 5.11 The Zero Crossings button on the toolbar adjusts your selection inward to the closest available zero crossing points.

Snapping Your Selections

To make selection a little easier, you may want to enable *snapping*, which causes selection boundaries to adjust themselves to align with cues, zero crossing points, or other markers. Also known as *snap to grid*, snapping is a feature common to many audio and video editing tools and is helpful for adding precision to your work.

You can enable or disable snapping by choosing Edit > Snapping or right-clicking the timeline and selecting Snapping (**Figure 5.12**).

The Snapping menu offers these options:

◆ **Snap to Cues:** Enables snapping to cue points (see "Using Cues" later in this chapter for information on cue points and ranges).

◆ **Snap to Ruler (Coarse):** Enables snapping to only the major numeric division markers in the timeline.

◆ **Snap to Ruler (Fine):** Enables snapping to any division markers in the timeline.

◆ **Snap to Zero Crossings:** Enables snapping to the nearest zero crossing point.

◆ **Snap to Frames (Always):** Enables snapping to frame boundaries if the time format is set to Frames.

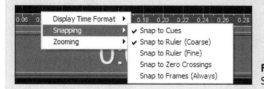

Figure 5.12 Right-click the timeline and select Snapping to access snapping-related options.

Using the Zoom Controls

When you're working on a waveform or a multitrack project, you'll often want to zoom in on the exact part of the display that you're working on for the utmost precision. You can find all the zoom tools you need in the Zoom window (**Figure 5.13**). If you don't see the Zoom window, choose Window > Zoom Controls to check the option (unchecking it will hide the window again), or click the Hide/Show Zoom Controls button (**Figure 5.14**).

◆ The **Zoom In Horizontally** button automatically zooms in on the center of the open waveform (in Edit view) or session (in Multitrack view).

◆ The **Zoom Out Horizontally** button zooms out from the center of the open waveform or session. (If you cannot zoom out any farther, this button will be dimmed.)

◆ The **Zoom In Vertically** button makes the open waveform taller in Edit view. In Multitrack view, it decreases the number of tracks visible in the Display window.

◆ The **Zoom Out Vertically** button makes the open waveform shorter in Edit view. In Multitrack view, it increases the number of tracks visible in the Display window.

◆ The **Zoom to Selection** button zooms in on the currently selected portion of a waveform or multitrack project.

◆ The **Zoom In to Right Edge of Selection** button zooms in on the right side of the currently highlighted selection.

◆ The **Zoom In to Left Edge of Selection** button zooms in on the left side of the currently highlighted selection.

◆ The **Zoom Out Full Both Axis** button zooms out completely, so that all of the waveform or multitrack session information is visible in the Display window.

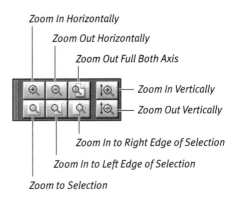

Zoom In Horizontally
Zoom Out Horizontally
Zoom Out Full Both Axis
Zoom In Vertically
Zoom Out Vertically
Zoom In to Right Edge of Selection
Zoom In to Left Edge of Selection
Zoom to Selection

Figure 5.13 The Zoom window contains all the zooming tools you need.

Figure 5.14 The Hide/Show Zoom Controls button on the toolbar.

✔ Tip

■ You can also zoom in or out by rolling the mouse over the right or left side of the horizontal scroll bar (you'll see the a special zoom cursor) and then dragging to the left or right.

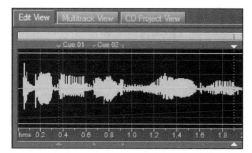

Figure 5.15 Cues are marked by triangular markers at the top and bottom of the Display window.

Figure 5.16 Right-click a cue pointer to access the Go to Cue List.

Figure 5.17 The Cue List window.

Using Cues

You may find it helpful when editing files in Edit view to use cues as signposts in your file. Audition allows you to choose and define cues in any way that you find helpful. You can mark an exact point in the file as a cue; this is called a *point cue*. You can also specify a range with specific start and end points as a cue; this is called a *range cue*.

Your cues are marked with triangular pointers at the top and bottom of the Display window (**Figure 5.15**). In the figure, Cue 1 is a point cue, and Cue 2 is a range cue. A point cue has a red pointer, and a range cue has a red pointer at the start point and a blue one at the end point. You can change a point cue to a range cue, or vice versa, by right-clicking a cue pointer and selecting Make Range or Make Point.

To list and edit your cues:

1. Display a list of your cues *by doing one of the following:*

   ▲ Choose Window > Cue List, right-click one of the cue pointers, and select Go to Cue List (**Figure 5.16**).

   ▲ Press Alt+8.

   A list of your cues and the point (or start and end points) in time that they specify appears in the Cue List window (**Figure 5.17**).

   continues on next page

continues on next page

USING CUES

55

2. Click the Edit Cue Info button to activate an editing window (**Figure 5.18**). Here you can rename your cue, add information to the Description field, and select from the four cue types:

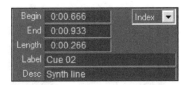

Figure 5.18 After you click the Edit Cut Info button in the Cue List window, you can edit, name, and enter descriptions of your cues.

- ▲ **Basic:** Allows you to mark important sections of a file that you may want to refer to later (for example, to mark a section you'll need to remove later, or the entry of a particular vocal or instrumental line).

- ▲ **Beat:** Functions just like the basic cue type, except that it's used to mark beats. This type of cue is particularly useful when working with percussion tracks that you want to loop. (To have Audition automatically locate and mark as beat cues the beats in your file, choose Edit > Auto-Cue > Find Beats and Mark.)

Figure 5.19 To change a cue's type, right-click one of its pointers, choose Change Cue Type, and select a type from the menu.

- ▲ **Track:** Marks a track split for a CD project.

- ▲ **Index:** Marks an index point for a track in a CD project.

To move cues:

- ◆ To move a cue, *do one of the following:*
  - ▲ Drag the cue pointer to a new location. (If it's a range cue, use the red start-point pointer.)
  - ▲ Open the Cue List window and manipulate the values to make adjustments.

To delete cues:

- ◆ To delete a single cue, right-click a pointer and select Delete.

- ◆ To delete more than one cue at a time, open the Cue List window, select the appropriate cues, and click the Del button.

✔ Tips

- ■ You can also change a cue's type by right-clicking a cue pointer and selecting Change Cue Type (**Figure 5.19**).

- ■ To preserve your cues when you save your audio file, be sure to select Save Extra Non-Audio Information in the Save As dialog box.

USING CUES

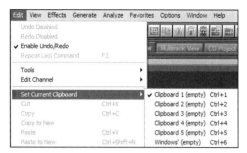

Figure 5.20 Choose Edit > Set Current Clipboard to choose among Audition's five clipboards or select the Windows clipboard.

Copying and Cutting Audio

Among the most basic and common audio-editing tasks are copying and cutting audio content. You might copy or cut to move audio content to another location or file, for instance, or you might use the cut functionality to trim unneeded sections from a waveform.

When you copy or cut audio in Edit view, Audition saves it on one of its five clipboards. Think of these as supercharged versions of the standard Windows clipboard: they work the same way but they can handle more data more quickly.

Audition allows multiple clipboards because users may want to have several different audio clips ready to paste at any given time. Clipboard 1 is selected by default; if you copy something to Clipboard 1 and then fail to choose another clipboard before copying something else, the audio you copied to Clipboard 1 originally will be replaced.

To choose a clipboard:

1. Choose Edit > Set Current Clipboard.

   The Clipboard pop-up menu opens (**Figure 5.20**).

2. Choose one of the five numbered Audition clipboards.

✔ Tip

- In cases where you want to copy audio data from Audition and paste it into another application, choose the Windows clipboard.

To copy audio:

1. Make a selection, or deselect everything if you want to copy the entire waveform.

2. Choose Edit > Copy (**Figure 5.21**), press Ctrl+C, or click the Copy button in the toolbar (**Figure 5.22**).

   Audition copies the selection to the clipboard, leaving the original in place.

To copy and paste in one step:

◆ Choose Edit > Copy to New.

   This brings your copied material into a new window.

✔ Tip

■ You can access the same Cut, Copy, and Paste commands as are on the Edit menu by right-clicking your selection (or deselected complete waveform) in the Display window.

To cut audio:

1. Make a selection, or deselect everything if you want to cut the entire waveform.

2. Choose Edit > Cut, press Ctrl+X, or click the Cut button on the toolbar (**Figure 5.23**).

   Audition cuts the selection and copies it to the clipboard, removing the selection from its original location.

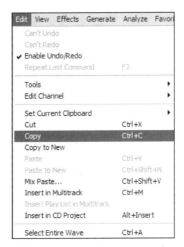

Figure 5.21 Options for copying audio can be accessed from the Edit menu.

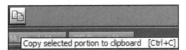

Figure 5.22 Click the Copy button on the toolbar to copy audio in a waveform.

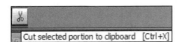

Figure 5.23 Click the Cut button on the toolbar to remove audio from a waveform and place it on your selected clipboard.

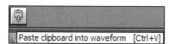

Figure 5.24 Click the Paste button on the toolbar to paste audio into a waveform.

Pasting Audio

In Edit view, the Paste command brings the data in the currently selected clipboard into the currently open waveform. The data will be converted, if necessary, to the same format as the waveform into which you are pasting it.

If you use the Paste to New option, the new waveform inherits the format, sample rate, and other characteristics of the original data.

To paste audio in the current waveform:

1. Place the cursor at the point in the waveform where you want the audio to appear, or select the audio that you want the new audio to replace.

2. Choose Edit > Paste, press Ctrl+V, or click the Paste button on the toolbar (**Figure 5.24**).

To paste the audio on the clipboard into a new file:

◆ Choose Edit > Paste to New or press Ctrl+Shift+N.

✔ Tip

■ If you want the pasted data to be high-lighted after it's brought into your wave-form, make sure the Highlight After Paste check box is selected on the General tab of the Options > Settings window (**Figure 5.25**).

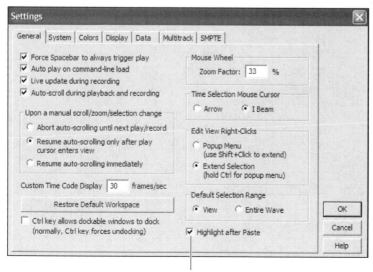

Highlight After Paste

Figure 5.25 The Highlight After Paste option on the General tab of the Options > Settings window auto-matically highlights newly pasted audio in a waveform.

PASTING AUDIO

Using the Mix Paste command

The Mix Paste command allows you to superimpose one piece of audio on top of another. You may want to do this to combine two different snare-drum sounds for a nice, thick whack, for example, or to add a harmony vocal part to an existing lead.

In most cases, a multitrack session is a better environment for executing such tasks, but when you want a quick and easy way to blend sounds in Edit view, the Mix Paste command may prove handy.

To mix paste audio:

1. Cut or copy the desired audio to the currently selected clipboard, with your existing waveform open.

2. Choose Edit > Mix Paste.

3. Press Ctrl+Shift+V or click the Mix Paste button on the toolbar (**Figure 5.26**).

The Mix Paste window appears, with several settings for you to configure (**Figure 5.27**):

1. **Volume**: Move the sliders or adjust the percentage (0 to 100) to change the volume of the left and right stereo channels.

2. **Invert**: Check the box to turn the waveform of the corresponding channel upside-down.

3. **Lock Left/Right**: Check the box to lock the left- and right-channel sliders so that they move in tandem.

4. **Insert**: Select this to paste your audio in the current cursor location; if you make a selection, your pasted audio will replace the selection.

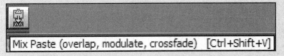

Mix Paste (overlap, modulate, crossfade)   [Ctrl+Shift+V]

Figure 5.26 Click the Mix Paste button on the toolbar to blend the audio clip on the clipboard with the audio in a waveform.

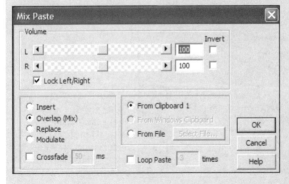

Figure 5.27 The Mix Paste window allows you to configure the options for blending two audio clips.

continues on next page

PASTING AUDIO

Using the Mix Paste command *(continued)*

5. **Overlap (Mix)**: Select this to mix the audio you're pasting with the current waveform.

6. **Replace**: Select this to replace the audio in the current waveform with the audio you're pasting, starting at the current cursor point.

7. **Modulate**: Select this to overlap, but with modulation added for an unusual effect.

8. **Crossfade**: Check this box to fade your pasted audio in at the beginning, and out at the end. Select a value in milliseconds to specify the duration of the fades.

9. **From Clipboard [Number]**: Check here to make sure you're about to paste audio from the proper Audition clipboard.

10. **From Windows Clipboard**: Select this if you're pasting something from the Windows clipboard, for instance audio copied from another application (this is disabled if nothing is in the Windows clipboard).

11. **From File**: Select this if you're pasting from a file; click Select File to browse to the file.

12. **Loop Paste**: Check this box if you want your pasted audio to repeat; you can specify the number of times.

PASTING AUDIO

Deleting Audio

Deleting audio is different from cutting it in that the audio is not moved to a clipboard and therefore is not available for pasting. You can get deleted audio back only by choosing Edit > Undo, or File > Revert to Saved as long as you haven't saved your file since the deletion was made.

You can select and delete specific parts of your waveform, or make a selection and trim away the parts of the waveform that are not selected.

To delete audio:

1. Make a selection in the waveform.

2. Choose Edit > Delete Selection (**Figure 5.28**), press the Delete key on your keyboard or click the Delete button on the toolbar (**Figure 5.29**).

To trim deselected audio:

1. Make a selection in the waveform containing the audio that you want to keep.

2. Choose Edit > Trim, press Ctrl+T, or click the Trim button on the toolbar (**Figure 5.30**).

Figure 5.28 Choose Edit > Delete Selection to remove the selected audio from a waveform.

Figure 5.29 Click the Delete button on the toolbar to remove audio from a waveform.

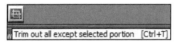

Figure 5.30 Click the Trim button on the toolbar to remove all nonselected audio from a waveform.

DELETING AUDIO

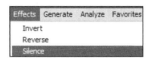

Figure 5.31 Choose Effects ›
Silence to replace the selected
audio in a waveform with a
silent clip of the same length.

Adding or Removing Silence

Sometimes, you may want to add silence to an audio file. Whether you want to mute part of your waveform and replace it with a silent pause of the same length, or insert a specific amount of new silence in the middle of the waveform, Audition makes the job easy.

There are two ways to add silence to your waveform: replacing an existing section with silence, but keeping the duration the same; or inserting several seconds or more of silence into the waveform, which increases its overall length by the duration of the insertion.

Removing silence, which you may want to do to trim track length, is easy, too. Let's say you're editing a waveform of a radio interview. The time limit for the piece is 5 minutes, yet the interview file runs 45 seconds longer than that. What can you do to shorten the waveform to 5 minutes without losing any of the content?

Audition can detect and remove instances of silence within a waveform. As part of the process, you can configure the program to specify exactly what constitutes removable silence within the file.

To replace an existing section with silence:

1. Make a selection in the waveform to specify the audio you want replaced with silence.

2. Choose Effects > Silence (**Figure 5.31**). The selection you made will be replaced by a silent passage of the same length.

To insert a specific duration of silence in a waveform:

1. Place your cursor at the point in the waveform where you want to insert the silence. (You can also make a selection if you want to remove a piece of audio at the same time.)

2. Choose Generate > Silence (**Figure 5.32**).

3. In the Generate Silence window (**Figure 5.33**), specify the length, in seconds, of the silent passage you want to insert.

4. Click OK.

   A stretch of silence of the specified duration appears at your chosen insertion point.

To remove silence from a waveform:

1. Make a selection in the waveform to specify the part from which you want silent segments removed. If you want to remove silence from the entire waveform, leave it deselected.

2. Choose Edit > Delete Silence.

3. In the Delete Silence window (**Figure 5.34**), configure the available options:

   ▲ **"Silence" is defined as:** Enter a decibel value in the Signal is Below box to configure the maximum level that should be recognized as silence. Also, specify a millisecond value in the For More Than box to configure how long that level should be sustained to be recognized as silence.

   ▲ **"Audio" is defined as:** Enter a decibel value in the Signal is Above box to configure the minimum level that should be recognized as audio. Also, specify a millisecond value in the For More Than box to configure how long that level should be sustained to be recognized as audio.

Figure 5.32 Choose Generate > Silence to insert a new silent clip at a particular point in a waveform.

Figure 5.33 Specify the desired length of the new silent clip in the Generate Silence window.

Figure 5.34 Use the Delete Silence window to set up automatic deletion of silent clips in a waveform.

▲ **Find Levels:** Click this button to have Audition scan your selection and suggest values for the signal levels.

▲ **Mark Deletions in Cue List:** Check this box to have the points in the waveform where silence is removed added to the cue list.

▲ **Limit Continuous Silence to:** Specify a minimum value in milliseconds to keep in your file. For example, if you set 100 milliseconds, silences shorter than that will be left alone, and those longer than that will be shortened to 100 milliseconds.

▲ **Scan for Silence Now:** Click this button to see how many silences will be removed when you click OK, and their total duration.

4. Click OK.

The silence is removed.

ADDING OR REMOVING SILENCE

Changing Sample Type

As we saw in Chapter 2, the sample rate of an audio file is a value that represents the number of frequencies that can be encoded in the file. You can change the sample rate and channel format (mono or stereo) of an open waveform at any time in Edit view.

If you're unsure about how such a change will affect the sound of your audio, you can preview the change before destructively editing your audio file.

Once you're satisfied with a new sample rate as previewed, you can go ahead and make the change.

To preview a sample rate change:

1. Choose Edit > Adjust Sample Rate (**Figure 5.35**).

2. In the Adjust Sample Rate window (**Figure 5.36**), select one of the given sample rates or enter a value of your own in the Sample Rate field.

3. Click OK.

✔ Tip

- Make sure you select a value your sound card can handle. Choose Options > Device Properties to check your sound card's capabilities.

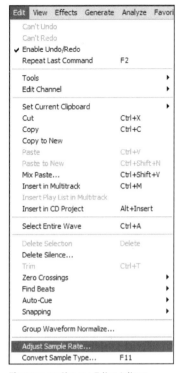

Figure 5.35 Choose Edit > Adjust Sample Rate to preview a sample-rate change.

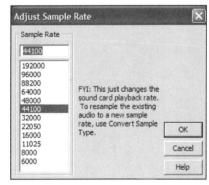

Figure 5.36 The Adjust Sample Rate window.

Figure 5.37 Click the Convert Sample Type button on the toolbar to change sample- or bit-rate settings in a waveform.

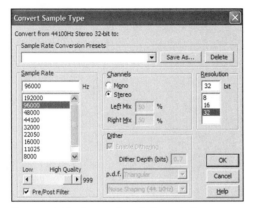

Figure 5.38 The Convert Sample Type window.

To change a waveform's sample rate:

1. Choose Edit > Convert Sample Type, press the F11 key on your keyboard, or click the Convert Sample Type button on the toolbar (**Figure 5.37**).

   The Convert Sample Type window opens (**Figure 5.38**).

2. In the Convert Sample Type window, select one of the given sample rates or enter a value of your own in the Sample Rate field.

3. Use the slider to adjust the quality of the sampling conversion.

4. Click OK.

   Audition changes the sample rate based on your selection and returns you to Edit view.

✔ Tip

- Adobe recommends using higher values, which takes longer but results in less high-frequency roll-off, when converting to a lower sample rate. When moving to a higher rate, the difference between high and low quality settings is much less apparent.

Changing Bit Depths

As we saw in Chapter 2, you'll get better-sounding audio if you record and edit at a high bit depth like 32-bit. However, when it comes time to use your audio in a practical application like transferring it to CD, for instance, you'll find you may need to change the bit depth first (a CD can only accommodate 16-bit audio). Thankfully, Audition makes this process a snap.

To change a waveform's bit depth:

1. Choose Edit > Convert Sample Type, press the F11 key on your keyboard, or click the Convert Sample Type button on the toolbar.

2. In the Convert Sample Type window, specify a bit depth in the Resolution list or enter a value of your own in the Bit field (Figure 5.38).

3. If you're converting to a lower bit depth, configure the settings in the Dither field as desired. (See Chapter 2 for a discussion of the dithering choices available here.)

4. Click OK.

   Audition changes the bit depth based on your selection and returns you to Edit view.

Converting Stereo and Mono

Often, a waveform imported from a video clip or other source will arrive as a single-channel, mono file. If you plan to output that file to CD or another medium capable of delivering two-channel audio, you may want to convert the file to stereo. Audition not only allows you to separate the audio into two channels; it also lets you set the amplitude of each channel and control your new stereo mix.

Conversely, if you're trying to conserve bandwidth or otherwise reduce file size, or if you have other plans for the left or right channel, you may want to convert the waveform to mono and squeeze all that two-channel audio into a single channel. Here, Audition also lets you set parameters for left- and right-channel amplitude before converting the waveform.

To convert mono to stereo, or vice versa:

1. Choose Edit > Convert Sample Type, press the F11 key on your keyboard, or click the Convert Sample Type button on the toolbar.

2. In the Convert Sample Type window, click either the Mono or Stereo button in the Channels field (Figure 5.38).

continues on next page

3. Specify the Left and Right Mix options.

▲ When converting from mono to stereo, use the Left and Right Mix options to specify the amplitude of the mono file in each stereo channel. For example, a value of 90% in the Left Mix field and a value of 10% in the Right Mix field would result in a stereo file in which the sound would appear to be coming mostly from the left channel.

▲ When converting from stereo to mono, use the Left and Right Mix options to specify the prominence each stereo channel will have in the new mono "mix" you're creating. For optimal balance, you'll usually want to use an even 50/50 split for these values.

USING
EFFECTS

After you've recorded and edited your audio files, you may want to sweeten, distort, tweak, or otherwise make them more interesting with effects. Adobe Audition offers an impressive range of effects, from reverbs and delays to phase-shifting, flanging, and various other filters.

In this chapter, I'll show you how to use presets to store, customize, and access your commonly used effects, and how you can preview effects before you apply them. You'll see how many effects allow you to fine-tune them by using a graphic interface. To introduce you to the range of effects you will be applying and tweaking and show you how they may affect your recordings, I'll take you on a whirlwind tour through many of the individual effects in the Effects submenus. Finaly, I'll walk you through the configuration of three frequently used effects.

Configuring Effects

Almost all the effects in Audition are configurable, which means that you don't just apply them—you tell Audition how, when, and where to apply them and to what degree. You configure some effects with a scrubber bar, some by changing numerical settings, and others by manipulating graphs. You can configure effects for specific, one-time uses or, in some cases, create preset configurations that will be applied each time you use a given effect.

Once you know what the effects are and have mastered the controls for fine-tuning them, you will know how to use effects in Audition. Keep in mind that with many effects, a little goes a long way, so be sure to use them judiciously.

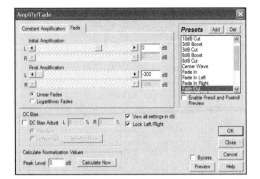

Figure 6.1 The Amplify/Fade window contains a selection of presets that you can modify or use as is; you can also add your own presets.

Using and Creating Presets

Some of the effects in Audition allow you to use and create presets, which can store frequently used settings for later access. The program installs a number of its own presets by default; you can use these or come up with your own. You can always preview effects, and you can remove any effect you apply by using the Undo command. Feel free to experiment until you find the setting you want.

In the following examples, I use the Amplify/Fade effect to illustrate how presets work. First I apply one of the program's default presets to fade out the end of an audio clip that's open in Edit view, and then I show you how to create a custom preset of your own. Finally, I explain how to modify or delete an existing preset.

To fade out an audio clip using an existing preset:

1. In the Display window in Edit view, select the portion of the clip that you want to fade out. (If you want the fade to encompass the entire clip, either select or deselect the entire clip. See Chapter 5 for more on how to select and deselect clips.)

2. Choose Effects > Amplitude > Amplify/Fade.
   The Amplify/Fade window opens (**Figure 6.1**).

3. In the Presets box, select Fade Out.
   The settings stored in the preset are shown in the other parts of the dialog box. If necessary, you can fine-tune these settings before you apply the preset.

continues on next page

4. Click OK.

The default Fade Out preset creates a fade by lowering the amplification of the selected audio signal from 0dB to −300dB over the span of the clip. In effect, the preset fades the audio out completely. In the next example, I show you how to create a custom preset that is similar but fades the amplification down to −100dB.

To create a custom preset:

1. In the Display window in Edit view, select the audio to which you want to apply the effect.

2. Choose Effects > Amplitude > Amplify/Fade.

The Amplify/Fade window opens.

3. On the Fade tab, specify the settings that you want to save in the new preset. In this example, set Initial Amplification to 0dB and Final Amplification to −100dB.

4. In the Presets box, click the Add button.

The Add Presets dialog box opens.

5. Enter a name for the new preset (**Figure 6.2**).

6. Click OK.

The new preset now appears in the list in the Presets box (**Figure 6.3**).

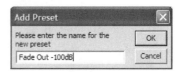

Figure 6.2 The Add Presets window allows you to customize and name your custom presets.

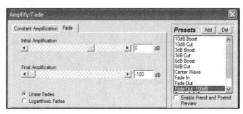

Figure 6.3 The Presets box contains a list of all of an effect's available presets.

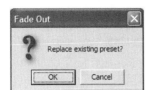

Figure 6.4 When you modify a preset, the program asks you to verify that you want to replace the earlier version.

To modify a preset:

1. Select the preset in the Presets list.

2. Modify the settings as you wish.

3. In the Presets box, click the Add button.

4. Reenter the name of the preset as it already exists.

5. Click OK.

   A window opens asking if you want to replace the existing preset (**Figure 6.4**).

6. Click OK.

To delete a preset:

1. Select the preset in the Presets list.

2. In the Presets box, click the Del button.

   A window opens asking if you're sure you want to delete the preset.

3. Click Yes.

USING AND CREATING PRESETS

Previewing Effects

You can preview an effect before you apply it to hear how it's going to sound.

If you're adding an effect to a small part of a larger clip, you can configure and add preroll and postroll durations to the preview. This extends the preview with a small amount of the audio just prior to and just after the selected clip, so that you can listen to the transition between the segment with the effect added and the unaffected audio just before and after it.

To preview an effect:

1. In the effect window that you have open, click the Preview button (**Figure 6.5**).
   Your selected audio clip will begin looping over and over, with the current effect settings applied.

2. Adjust the effect settings as you desire. You will hear the your adjustments as the clip continues to loop.

3. Click Stop to end the preview.

✔ Tip

■ While you're previewing an effect, check the Bypass box to hear the original audio without the effect added. This provides an easy way to compare your processed audio to the original clip.

To configure preroll and postroll durations:

1. Right-click either the Play or Play to End button in the Transport Control window.

2. Select Preroll and Postroll Options (**Figure 6.6**).
   The Preroll and Postroll Options window appears (**Figure 6.7**).

Figure 6.5 Click the Preview button to hear an effect before you apply it.

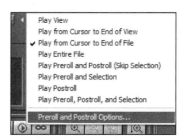

Figure 6.6 Right-click either the Play or Play to End button to enable preroll and postroll options.

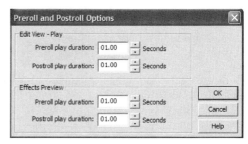

Figure 6.7 Set options for preroll and postroll previewing in the Preroll and Postroll Options window.

Figure 6.8 You can enable preroll and postroll preview on the Effects menu.

Figure 6.9 You can also enable preroll and postroll preview via a check box in each effect's window.

3. In the Effects Preview fields, enter the desired preroll and postroll durations, measured in seconds.

4. Click OK.

To hear preroll and postroll durations during effects preview:

1. Do one of the following:

▲ Choose Effects > Enable Preroll and Postroll Preview (**Figure 6.8**).

▲ If there are presets for the effect you're using, check the Enable Preroll and Postroll Preview check box under the Presets list in the effect's dialog box (**Figure 6.9**).

2. Click the Preview button to hear your processed clip with preroll and postroll durations added.

PREVIEWING EFFECTS

Using Graphic Controls

When you access the various effects on the Effects menu, you'll see a number of different ways to manipulate the settings. In many cases, you enter values in fields. In others, you use levers, or *scrubbers*, to change settings (**Figure 6.10**).

In addition, some effects offer graphs in which you can configure your settings (**Figure 6.11**). In these graphs, you can create and move control points to fine-tune the effect to your specifications. (In most cases, you can click a Preview button to hear how what you're doing is affecting the selected audio clip.)

The lines between your control points will usually appear as straight lines, unless there's a Splines option available and you select it (**Figure 6.12**). This creates a curve that follows your control points across the graph, resulting in smoother transitions between various points in the arc of the applied effect.

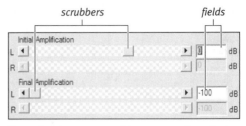

Figure 6.10 Levers, or *scrubbers*, are used to adjust the settings for some effects.

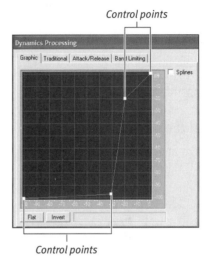

Figure 6.11 You can use control points in a graphic interface to adjust the parameters of some effects.

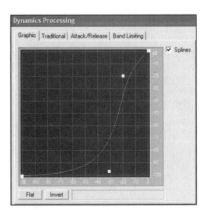

Figure 6.12 When a Splines option is available, you can select it to create smoother transitions between control points in a graph.

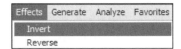

Figure 6.13 Choose Effects > Invert to turn a waveform upside down.

Effects Menu Options

The Effects menu contains an impressive array of audio effects. Two of the simplest are at the very top: the Invert and Reverse commands.

The Invert tool turns your waveform upside down: positive dB values become negative, and vice-versa. You can use this tool to correct an out-of-phase left or right channel in a stereo clip or to create phasing effects.

The Reverse tool simply turns your audio clip back-to-front so that you can hear it backwards. Backwards sounds have been used as special effects in recordings dating back to the 1960s; almost any sound will deliver an intriguing variation of itself when played backwards.

To invert an audio clip:

1. Select the audio you want to invert.

2. Choose Effects > Invert (**Figure 6.13**). Audition inverts the dB values for the selected clip.

To reverse an audio clip:

1. Select the audio you want to reverse.

2. Choose Effects > Reverse. Audition reverses the audio for the selected clip.

The Effects submenus

The six submenus of the Effects menu (**Figure 6.14**) provide a varied palette of manipulations, distortions, and effects for your audio. In this section, we'll look at five of these submenus and the options they offer. (The sixth, Noise Reduction, will be covered in Chapter 11.)

Figure 6.14
The Effects menu contains six submenus.

✔ Tip

- In each case, if you have preset values for the effect you're configuring (such as Noisy Hot Guitar) in the Dynamics Processing example, you can simply choose the preset if that's your desired effect instead of configuring the effect manually each time. The preset values will appear, and you can tweak those as required for the clip you're working on.

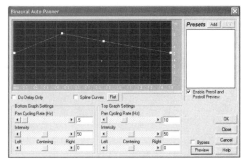

Figure 6.15 The Binaural Auto-Panner window.

Amplitude submenu options

- **Amplify/Fade** Allows adjustments to the volume of an audio clip. See the section "Configuring Frequently Used Effects" later in this chapter for an in-depth look at configuring the Amplify/Fade effect.

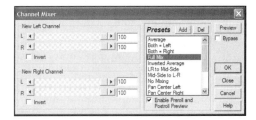

Figure 6.16 The Channel Mixer window.

- **Binaural Auto-Panner (Figure 6.15):** Lets you delay each channel in a stereo file at differing rates to create the illusion of sound moving from one side of the stereo image to another over time. This effect (formerly known as "Brainwave Synchronizer" in Audition's reckless youth as Cool Edit Pro) is especially helpful to users who are working with audio for video projects, and may want to create surround sound-type effects in stereo files by mapping sound movement to movement in the video.

- **Channel Mixer (Figure 6.16):** Lets you manipulate the balance of a stereo clip. You can mix the original left and right

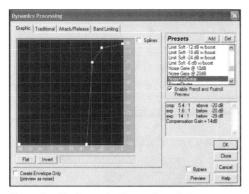

Figure 6.17 The Dynamics Processing window.

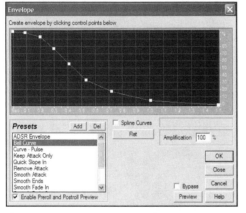

Figure 6.18 The Envelope window.

Figure 6.19 The Hard Limiting window.

channels together at various ratios to create new left and right channels, which can result in interesting stereo effects.

◆ **Dynamics Processing (Figure 6.17):** Enables the expansion or compression of perceived dynamic range, or the width of the gulf between the loudest and softest sounds in your clip. You can lower the volume of a clip's loudest points to match more closely the volume of the remainder. You can also lower the volume of the softest points to exaggerate the clip's dynamic range.

◆ **Envelope (Figure 6.18):** Provides a graph that allows you to plot multiple amplitude changes over the course of an audio clip. A point at the top of the graph represents 100% amplitude, or full volume, while a point at the bottom represents silence.

◆ **Hard Limiting (Figure 6.19):** Lets you reduce the amplitude of audio peaks above a certain level (measured in decibels) without affecting audio below that level. This reduces the perceived dynamic range but increases the perceived loudness of the audio clip as a whole. This effect would be particularly useful before you convert a 32-bit audio file to 16-bit, because, without it, louder audio recorded at 32 bits tends to clip (distort) when downsampled to 16-bit. In the Clipping Statistics section of this window, Audition lets you know if you've successfully removed any clipping from the hard-limited portion of the waveform.

continues on next page

EFFECTS MENU OPTIONS

- **Normalize (Figure 6.20):** Reduces the amplitude of an entire audio clip so that its loudest points do not cause distortion. This differs from Hard Limiting in that it does not reduce the dynamic range; the loudest points are made softer so as not to distort, and the quietest points are reduced in volume to maintain the original loudness-to-softness ratio.

- **Pan/Expand (Figure 6.21):** Allows you to change the relationship between the left and right channels of a stereo audio clip. When a sound appears at the same amplitude in both the left and right channels, we usually perceive it to be in the center of the stereo picture. This phantom center channel can be manipulated using the Pan/Expand effect; in essence, you can pan it just as you would a right or left channel to create interesting stereo effects. You can also use this effect to narrow or widen the overall stereo image.

- **Stereo Field Rotate (Figure 6.22):** Allows you to rotate the perceived stereo field over time. For example, over the course of a one-minute audio clip, you can slowly rotate the stereo field so that the instruments in the left channel at the beginning have "moved" to the right channel by the end, and vice versa.

Delay Effects submenu options

- **Chorus (Figure 6.23):** Creates the illusion of several voices or instruments playing where just one existed in the original clip. The program blends the original signal with slight variations of itself, depending on the settings chosen. Chorus is often used to thicken or add texture and personality to rather plain sounds.

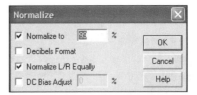

Figure 6.20 The Normalize window.

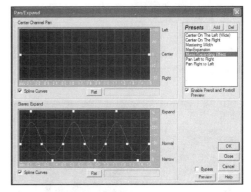

Figure 6.21 The Pan/Expand window.

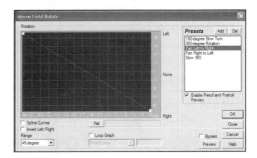

Figure 6.22 The Stereo Field Rotate window.

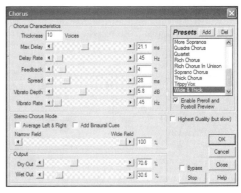

Figure 6.23 The Chorus window.

EFFECTS MENU OPTIONS

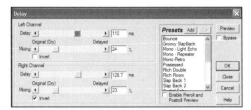

Figure 6.24 The Delay window.

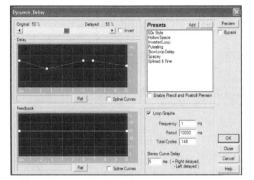

Figure 6.25 The Dynamic Delay window.

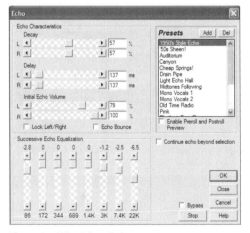

Figure 6.26 The Echo window.

◆ **Delay (Figure 6.24):** Adds a delayed repeat, or echo, to the original signal. You can adjust the delay time for a wide variety of echo effects. Especially short delay times can provide an artificial double-tracking or chorus-like effect, while longer delay times sound more like a single echo.

◆ **Dynamic Delay (Figure 6.25):** Allows you to change the delay settings over the course of an audio clip.

◆ **Echo (Figure 6.26):** Provides a delayed repeat of the original signal, like the Delay effect but with the option to repeat the echo a number of times at declining amplitudes. The echoes repeat more and more softly until they fade away. You can create some ear-catching effects by altering the delay times, equalization, and separate left- and right-channel settings of the echoes.

continues on next page

EFFECTS MENU OPTIONS

◆ **Echo Chamber (Figure 6.27):** Allows you to create the illusion of sound existing in chambers or rooms through the use of complex combinations of echoes to simulate various types of room reflections. To configure the series of echoes required, you can enter the dimensions of your virtual room and the locations in that room of the virtual microphones that are capturing the sound.

◆ **Flanger (Figure 6.28):** Similar to the Chorus effect; adds to an existing signal a phased, time-delayed version of itself. Flanging was pioneered during the first days of psychedelic rock in the 1960s (some rock historians have claimed that John Lennon of the Beatles coined the term *flanging* during sessions at Abbey Road Studios) and continues to be a popular effect associated with such music.

◆ **Full Reverb:** Similar to the regular Reverb effect (described later). As with many of the effects you apply in Audition (especially the more processor-intensive ones), you have to wait a few seconds for Audition to process the reverb you apply (**Figure 6.29**). For an in-depth look at configuring the Full Reverb effect, see the section "Configuring Frequently Used Effects" later in this chapter.

◆ **Multitap Delay (Figure 6.30):** Allows you to apply multiple delays to your sound clip, each with its own delay-time settings. You can put one delay inside another or have a series of delays with different feedback effects. You can also choose to equalize the delay sounds or apply them to just one channel of a stereo clip.

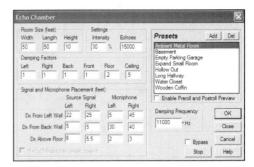

Figure 6.27 The Echo Chamber window.

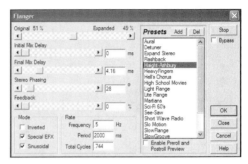

Figure 6.28 The Flanger window.

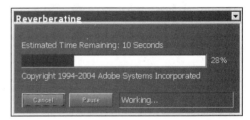

Figure 6.29 Audition pauses to render the reverb effect.

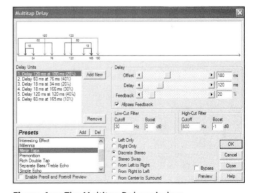

Figure 6.30 The Multitap Delay window.

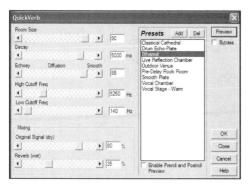

Figure 6.31 The QuickVerb window.

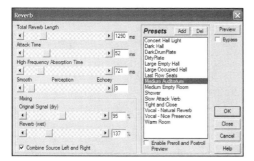

Figure 6.32 The Reverb window.

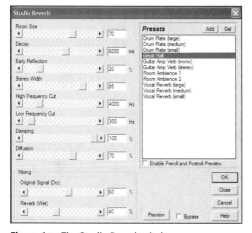

Figure 6.33 The Studio Reverb window.

◆ **QuickVerb (Figure 6.31):** Similar to the Reverb and Full Reverb effects, but simpler and easier on your computer processor. You'll find this effect handy when working on a multitrack session, where you'll often want to apply a reverb effect in real time without unduly taxing your system's resources.

◆ **Reverb (Figure 6.32):** Adds the illusion of reverberation in various types of rooms or acoustic spaces. This effect is easier to configure than the Full Reverb effect, but your options are comparatively limited.

◆ **Studio Reverb (Figure 6.33):** A new addition in Audition 1.5. Like QuickVerb, this effect offers faster and more processor-friendly reverb effects than Reverb and Full Reverb. However, although it offers better sound quality and more options than QuickVerb, you still get higher-quality sound with Reverb or Full Reverb.

continues on next page

EFFECTS MENU OPTIONS

♦ **Sweeping Phaser (Figure 6.34):**
Applies a phase-shifting effect to
your sound clip, similar to flanging.
(See Chapter 2 for information
about phase.)

Filters submenu options

♦ **Center Channel Extractor (Figure
6.35):** Reduces or removes audio information that is panned in the center
in a stereo sound clip, or reduces or
removes the audio that is *not* panned
center. One common use for this effect
is to remove the lead vocal, which is
usually panned in the center of modern
stereo mixes, to create karaoke-ready
instrumental tracks.

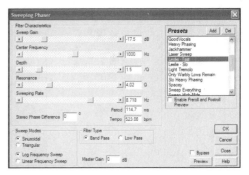

Figure 6.34 The Sweeping Phaser window.

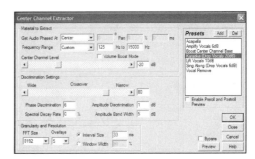

Figure 6.35 The Center Channel Extractor window.

Things to Keep in Mind When Using Reverb

You may use reverb for many different reasons. You may want to simulate the natural
ambience of a large concert hall or auditorium. You may want to add a prominent,
artificial-sounding reverb effect to a snare drum to recall the sounds of pop music of the
1980s (when such effects were highly fashionable). You may want to create an illusion of
space in a recording.

With the right reverb and panning effects in a multitrack mix, you can make a simple mono
acoustic guitar track sound like it exists in the room with the listener, even to the point of
creating the impression in the listener's mind that the guitarist is positioned to the left in a
large room.

Beware of adding too much reverb to an individual sound, particularly lead vocals and
instruments. Remember that an excessive amount can make the voice or instrument seem
distant in a mix. When you're working on an up-tempo song, keep the decay time (the
amount of time it takes for the reverberation to fade away) short; otherwise, your individual
parts may sound muddy and indistinct. Long decay times work well with slower material
and with classical music (in which emulating the long decay times typical of classical
concert halls may be desirable).

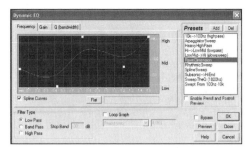

Figure 6.36 The Dynamic EQ window.

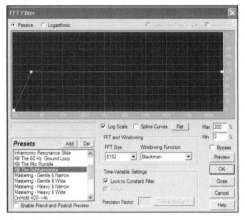

Figure 6.37 The FFT Filter window.

◆ **Dynamic EQ (Figure 6.36):** Allows you to apply different gain, frequency, and bandwidth settings to different sections of an audio clip.

◆ **FFT Filter (Figure 6.37):** Allows you to graphically create filters that reduce or boost particular frequencies. You can filter out all but a narrow band of frequencies to simulate the sound you hear over a telephone, for example, or all the frequencies below a certain threshold in an effort to eliminate low-frequency rumble.

◆ **Graphic Equalizer:** Allows you to adjust preset frequency bands with the aid of a graphic interface. See the section "Configuring Frequently Used Effects" later in this chapter for an in-depth look at configuring the Graphic Equalizer.

continues on next page

The Secret of Slapback Echo

Sun Records founder Sam Phillips pioneered an echo technique called *slapback* on Elvis Presley's first recording sessions, which was one of the characteristics that gave Elvis' early records such a haunting sound. Phillips achieved the effect in the control booth by using one console tape recorder and a second recorder mounted behind his head to provide a carefully calibrated tape delay.

Elvis' subsequent producers at RCA tried everything they could think of to duplicate the sound, including recording Elvis singing from the other end of the hall and even the bathroom at one point. But they never quite got the slapback echo, and Phillips never revealed the secret—at least not to RCA.

Thanks to digital recording programs like Audition, things are a little easier today. If you want to add slapback tape delay to your recordings and get an authentic Sun Studios rockabilly sound, choose the 1950s Style Echo preset or simply set the echo to 130 milliseconds (the magic number for slapback delay). Then learn to play guitar like Scotty Moore, and you'll be all set.

EFFECTS MENU OPTIONS

◆ **Graphic Phase Shifter (Figure 6.38):**
Allows adjustment of phase over the
course of an audio clip via a graphic
interface.

◆ **Notch Filter (Figure 6.39):** Enables you
to specify up to six frequency bands to
remove from your audio clip. This effect
is useful if you need to remove some very
narrow-frequency bands (such as a hum
or buzz at a specific frequency) without
adversely affecting others.

◆ **Parametric Equalizer (Figure 6.40):**
Allows you to make precise adjustments
to individual frequencies in a graphic
interface. Unlike the Graphic Equalizer,
which provides control only of preset
frequency bands, the Parametric
Equalizer enables you to single out
individual frequencies in an audio clip
for boosting, cutting, and/or filtering,
all at the same time.

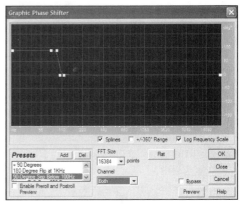

Figure 6.38 The Graphic Phase Shifter window.

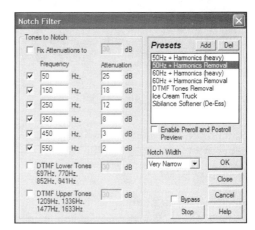

Figure 6.39 The Notch Filter window.

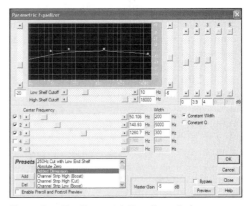

Figure 6.40 The Parametric Equalizer window.

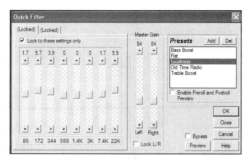

Figure 6.41 The Quick Filter window.

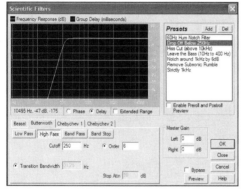

Figure 6.42 The Scientific Filters window.

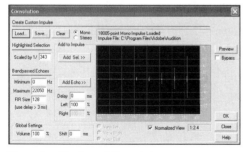

Figure 6.43 The Convolution window.

◆ **Quick Filter (Figure 6.41):** Provides an eight-band equalizer for general tone control, somewhat analogous to the bass, mid, and treble controls on home-audio equipment. The frequency values assigned to each band are general ones; adjusting the 1.4K band, for instance, also affects other frequencies close to that value.

◆ **Scientific Filters (Figure 6.42):** Allows high-pass, low-pass, and band-pass filtering. High-pass filtering attenuates low frequencies while passing high ones; low-pass filtering does the reverse. Band-pass filtering passes on frequency band and attenuates all of those above and below.

Special submenu options

◆ **Convolution (Figure 6.43):** Enables one audio clip to model the sound of another. For instance, you can blend a mono recording of your voice with a stereo recording of people clapping their hands in the middle of your favorite concert hall. The result will sound as if your voice had been captured in that same concert hall, as if you had been singing in the same spot where the handclaps occurred. This effect offers exciting possibilities and an interesting approach to adding echo, phase-shifting, and filtering effects to simple recorded sounds.

continues on next page

◆ **Distortion (Figure 6.44):** Adds distortion to your audio. You can simulate the sounds of blown speakers or amplifiers, fuzzy electric guitars, or overdriven recording consoles.

◆ **Music (Figure 6.45):** Allows you to use your selected audio clip as a voice as you create an original tune or harmony using the musical staff in the window. Simply drag the notes you want from the selection bar down into the staff and click the Listen button for a MIDI preview.

Time/Pitch submenu options

◆ **Doppler Shifter (Figure 6.46):** Edits your audio selection to simulate the decrease in pitch and tempo you hear as a speeding car approaches you and the increase you hear as it speeds away from you again.

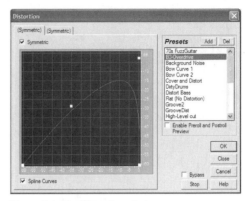

Figure 6.44 The Distortion window.

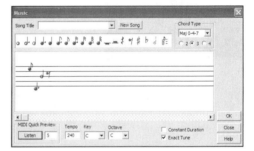

Figure 6.45 The Music window.

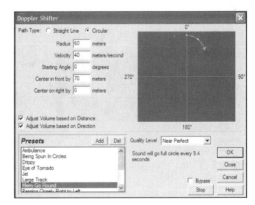

Figure 6.46 The Doppler Shifter window.

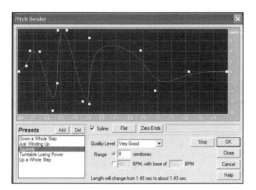

Figure 6.47 The Pitch Bender window.

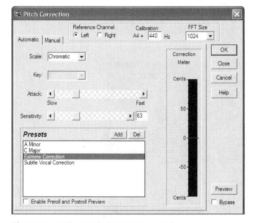

Figure 6.48 The Pitch Correction window.

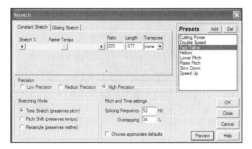

Figure 6.49 The Stretch window.

◆ **Pitch Bender (Figure 6.47):** Provides a graphic interface that allows you to adjust the pitch of your audio clip at various points. You can use this effect to simulate the sound of a turntable slowing down or to create a chord or harmony change that didn't exist in the original clip.

◆ **Pitch Correction (Figure 6.48):** Offers automatic and manual ways to correct or adjust the pitch of your selected audio. If you've recorded the greatest lead vocal of all time except for that one flat note at the very end, you can use this tool to fix your bum note and bring the performance that much closer to perfection.

◆ **Stretch (Figure 6.49):** Allows you to separate the tasks of changing pitch and tempo. For instance, you can transpose an audio clip to a higher key without speeding up the tempo. You can also boost the tempo of the clip without making your vocalist sound like Mickey Mouse. (You also have the option of changing both pitch and tempo at the same time.)

EFFECTS MENU OPTIONS

Configuring Frequently Used Effects

The effects in Adobe Audition's palette are too numerous to walk through the configuration process for each one here. In this section, however, we'll take an in-depth look at three effects (Full Reverb, Graphic Equalizer, and Amplify/Fade). This will accomplish two things: you'll see some of the various methods used in Audition to configure effects, and you'll get a close-up view of three of the effects you're most likely to use on a regular basis.

The Full Reverb effect simulates room reverberation to create the illusion of a sound originating in a particular place in relation to the listener. It offers a high degree of customization; you can specify the dimensions of your imaginary room and tweak the sound further via equalization.

The Graphic Equalizer effect allows you to cut or boost preset frequency bands with the aid of a graphic interface, which shows you a visual representation of the resulting EQ curve.

Finally, the Amplify/Fade effect allows adjustments to the volume of an audio clip, either consistently throughout the clip via the Constant Amplification tab or at a rising or falling rate to produce a fade via the Fade tab.

To apply the Full Reverb effect in the Edit View:

1. Make a selection in the waveform.

2. *Do one of the following:*
   - ▲ Choose Effects > Delay Effects > Full Reverb (**Figure 6.50**).
   - ▲ Click the Effects tab in the Organizer window, expand Delay Effects, and double-click Full Reverb (**Figure 6.51**).

   The Full Reverb window opens.

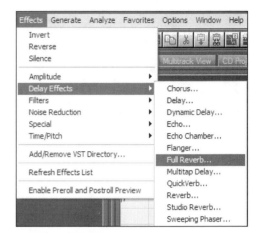

Figure 6.50 The Full Reverb effect can be found in Effects > Delay Effects.

Figure 6.51 You can also open the Full Reverb effect in the Effects tab of the Organizer window.

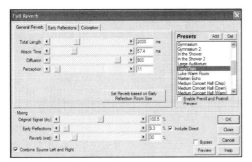

Figure 6.52 The Full Reverb window.

3. *Do any of the following:*

▲ Move the Original Signal (Dry) scrubber to adjust the prominence of the original signal relative to the reverb sound.

▲ Move the Early Reflections scrubber to adjust the perceived size of the virtual "room."

▲ Move the Reverb (Wet) scrubber to adjust the prominence of the reverb sound relative to the original signal.

▲ Check the Include Direct box to phase-shift the left and right channels of the original signal to best match the Early Reflections setting.

▲ Check the Combine Source Left and Right box to sum an original stereo signal to mono before the reverb is added.

4. Configure the options specific to each tab (see the following tasks).

5. Click OK.

   The Full Reverb effect is applied.

To configure the Full Reverb effect (General Reverb tab):

1. In the Full Reverb window, click the General Reverb tab (**Figure 6.52**).

2. *Do any of the following:*

▲ Set the Total Length scrubber, or enter a value in the adjacent field, to specify how many milliseconds the decay of the reverb should last.

▲ Set the Attack Time scrubber, or enter a value in the adjacent field, to specify how many milliseconds it should take for the reverb effect to reach maximum amplitude.

▲ Set the Diffusion scrubber, or enter a value in the adjacent field, to specify how many individual echoes should be contained in the reverb sound (higher settings result in smoother reverb).

▲ Raise the Perception setting, using either the scrubber or the adjacent value field, to increase the auditory perception that the reverb was produced naturally in a room (lower settings result in smoother but somewhat artificial-sounding reverb).

▲ Click the Set Reverb Based on Early Reflection Room Size button to set the Total Length and Attack Time settings to conform to the room-size settings configured in the Early Reflections tab (see the next task).

3. Go on to the next tab, or click OK.

To configure the Full Reverb effect (Early Reflections tab):

1. In the Full Reverb window, click the Early Reflections tab (**Figure 6.53**).

2. *Do any of the following:*

▲ Set the Room Size scrubber, or enter a value in the adjacent field, to specify the size of the room you want to emulate, in cubic meters.

▲ Set the Dimension scrubber, or enter a value in the adjacent field, to specify the virtual room's width-to-depth ratio.

▲ Set the Left/Right Location scrubber, or enter a percentage in the adjacent field, to move the virtual sound source (the original signal to which you're adding reverb) to a particular off-center location in the "room."

▲ Set the High Pass Cutoff scrubber, or enter a Hz value in the adjacent field, to avoid losing low-frequency (bassy) sounds below that value (the addition of reverb can often cause low-frequency loss due to phase issues).

3. Go on to the next tab, or click OK.

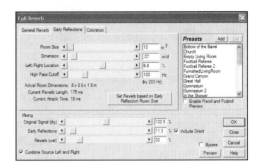

Figure 6.53 The Early Reflections tab of the Full Reverb window.

CONFIGURING FREQUENTLY USED EFFECTS

To configure the Full Reverb effect (Coloration tab):

1. In the Full Reverb window, click the Coloration tab (**Figure 6.54**).

2. *Do any of the following:*

   ▲ Move the three control points in the graph to color the reverb sound.

   ▲ Adjust the amplitude or frequency scrubbers to color the reverb sound.

   ▲ Adjust the values in the Hz and dB fields to color the reverb sound.

   ▲ Specify a value in the Q field to set the width of the mid band.

   ▲ Specify a value in the ms field to set the decay time for the affected reverb.

3. Click OK.

   The Full Reverb effect is applied.

✔ Tip

■ The *x*-axis of the graph shows frequency levels (Hz), which provide a way of equalizing the reverb sound. The *y*-axis shows amplitude in decibels (dB). There is one control point each for low, mid-range, and high frequencies; as you move them, you'll see the appropriate scrubber and field value change in real time.

CONFIGURING FREQUENTLY USED EFFECTS

Control points

Amplitude (dB) scrubbers

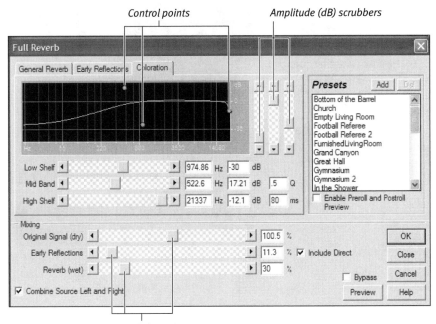

Frequency (Hz) scrubbers

Figure 6.54
The Coloration tab of the Full Reverb window.

To open the Graphic Equalizer effect in the Edit View:

1. Make a selection in the waveform.

2. *Do one of the following:*
   ▲ Choose Effects > Filters > Graphic Equalizer (**Figure 6.55**).
   ▲ Click the Effects tab in the Organizer window, expand Filters, and double-click Graphic Equalizer (**Figure 6.56**).
   The Graphic Equalizer window opens (**Figure 6.57**).

To configure the Graphic Equalizer effect:

1. *Do any of the following:*
   ▲ Click the 10 Bands, 20 Bands, or 30 Bands tab to specify how many frequency bands you wish to configure (use more bands if you want to exert control over more specific frequency ranges).
   ▲ Use a scrubber to boost or reduce the amplitude of the associated frequency range (your adjustments will be reflected in the graph).
   ▲ As an alternative to using the scrubbers, select a frequency band in the Band drop-down menu, and enter an amplitude value in dB in the Gain field.

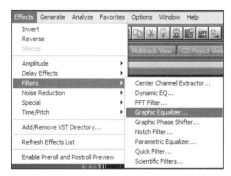

Figure 6.55 The Graphic Equalizer effect can be found in Effects › Filters.

Figure 6.56 You can also open the Graphic Equalizer effect in the Effects tab of the Organizer window.

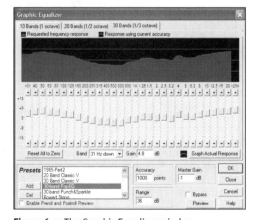

Figure 6.57 The Graphic Equalizer window.

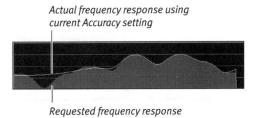

Actual frequency response using current Accuracy setting

Requested frequency response

Figure 6.58 When you click the Graph Actual Response button in the Graphic Equalizer window, a line is added to the graph to illustrate the actual frequency response that will result from the current Accuracy setting.

▲ Click the Graph Actual Response button to produce a green line in the graph representing the actual frequency adjustment that your equalization will produce. Compare it to the requested frequency adjustment, shown in blue in the graph (**Figure 6.58**). Increase the value in the Accuracy field as needed and click the button again until you're satisfied with the projected actual frequency adjustment.

▲ Click the Set All to Zero button at any time to return all equalization settings to 0 (to bring the waveform back to its unequalized state).

▲ Adjust the decibel value in the Range field to increase or decrease the amplitude range of the scrubbers.

▲ Adjust the decibel value in the Master Gain field if you need to compensate for volume changes that may result from your EQ settings.

2. Click OK.

The equalization is applied to the waveform.

To apply the Amplify/Fade effect in the Edit View:

1. Make a selection in the waveform.

2. *Do one of the following:*
   - ▲ Choose Effects > Amplitude > Amplify/Fade (**Figure 6.59**).
   - ▲ Click the Effects tab in the Organizer window, expand Amplitude, and double-click Amplify/Fade (**Figure 6.60**).

   The Amplify/Fade window opens.

3. *Do any of the following:*
   - ▲ Check the DC Bias Adjust box to adjust an off-center waveform (see Chapter 3 for information on DC bias).
   - ▲ Enter a value in the Peak Level field to specify a maximum amplitude for the normalization process. Click Calculate Now to scan the waveform and normalize based on that value.
   - ▲ Check the Lock Left/Right box to lock all L and R scrubbers together so that their settings always match; uncheck it if you want to use the scrubbers separately.
   - ▲ Check the View All Settings in dB box if you want amplitude settings to appear as decibel values; uncheck it if you want the settings represented as percentages of the original waveform values.

4. Configure the options specific to each tab (see the following tasks).

5. Click OK.

   The Amplify/Fade effect is applied.

Figure 6.59 The Amplify/Fade effect can be found in Effects > Amplitude.

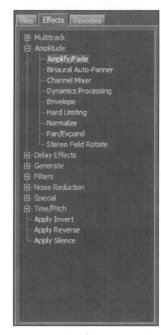

Figure 6.60
You can also open the Amplify/Fade effect in the Effects tab of the Organizer window.

CONFIGURING FREQUENTLY USED EFFECTS

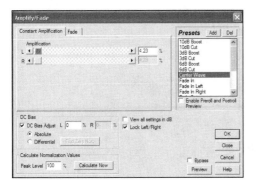

Figure 6.61 The Constant Amplification tab of the Amplify/Fade window.

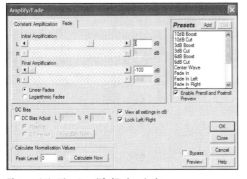

Figure 6.62 The Amplify/Fade window.

To configure the Amplify/Fade effect (Constant Amplification tab):

1. In the Amplify/Fade window, click the Constant Amplification tab (**Figure 6.61**).

2. Move the Amplification scrubbers, or enter values in the adjacent fields, to change the volume of the selected audio.

3. Go on to the next tab, or click OK.

To configure the Amplify/Fade effect (Fade tab):

1. In the Amplify/Fade window, click the Fade tab (**Figure 6.62**).

2. Use the scrubbers, or the adjacent fields, to choose amplitude values for Initial Amplification (the beginning of a fade) and Final Amplification (the end of a fade).

3. Check a button next to Linear Fades (for a smooth fade at a constant rate across your selection) or Logarithmic Fades (if you want a steeper slope at one end of the fade).

4. Click OK.

   The Amplify/Fade effect is applied.

✔ Tip

■ The Fade In and Fade Out presets in the Amplify/Fade effect window can be handy when editing files originating from vinyl records or live performances. You'll often want to fade LP clicks and pops or audience applause in and out at the beginning and end of such files, and these presets provide a quick and easy way to do it.

CONFIGURING FREQUENTLY USED EFFECTS

VST and DirectX Effects

With new features added in Audition 1.5, you can expand Audition's array of effects to include VST (Virtual Studio Technology) and DirectX plug-ins. If there's a particular effect you're looking for that Audition doesn't offer, try an Internet search for these types of plug-ins.

Once they're on your computer, adding the plug-ins to your Audition toolbox is easy. If you have Adobe Premiere Pro installed on the same machine, the VST plug-ins integrated into that video tool will automatically be made available in Audition; just choose Effects > VST to access them.

To enable other VST effects, choose Effects > Add/Remove VST Directory. In the window that opens, you can specify the folders on your computer that house the VST plug-ins. Then, every time you choose Effects > Refresh Effects List, Audition will scan those locations for new VST effects.

For DirectX effects, choose Effects > Enable DirectX Effects. (This option is available only if DirectX effects are not already enabled.) Audition will find any DirectX effects installed on your computer, and add them to the Effects > DirectX menu.

CONFIGURING FREQUENTLY USED EFFECTS

7

LOOPING SOUND

One of the basic building blocks of many types of modern music is the *loop*. You can take a short snippet of music or sound effects and repeat it over and over again so that it provides a beat or background upon which you can build a new composition.

Musicians and recording engineers used tape loops to generate repeating sounds as far back as the 1960s. Today, musicians are far more likely to create loops on computers. Rap, hip-hop, and alternative-rock musicians, especially, have done much to advance the art. They commonly use samples from other recordings as building blocks for their own records (after obtaining the necessary rights, of course).

People also create their own sounds and loop them, or use royalty-free sound files. Adobe Audition comes with a *Loopology* CD-ROM full of such files.

In this chapter, I'll discuss the different types of loops and how to create and customize them. I'll also explore how you can use loops in Audition to build or augment your own compositions.

Creating Loops

A loop is most often created from a file that contains one or two measures, or bars, of music. A typical modern song with a 4/4 time signature contains four beats in every bar. We'll use a two-bar, eight-beat sound example from the *Loopology* files to create a loop.

To create a loop from an existing file:

1. In Edit view, choose File > Open and locate the *Loopology* CD-ROM (**Figure 7.1**).

2. Open the Cel_Music_Beds folder and then the Funk_Beds_110BPM subfolder; then open the file 110bpmFunk02 (**Figure 7.2**).

3. To loop the entire two-bar sequence, open the Options menu, and select Loop Mode (**Figure 7.3**).

   You now have a smooth, seamlessly repeating loop. When you press the spacebar to listen to the file, you'll hear it play over and over again, giving you a continuous beat.

   Once you've selected and previewed your loop material, choose Edit > Copy to New. This copies your selection into a new file, in which you can fine-tune the loop properties.

✔ Tip

■ Groups like the Beatles pioneered the practice of sound-effects looping (listen to "Tomorrow Never Knows," from the 1966 album *Revolver*, for an early example). In Pink Floyd's "Money," from the 1973 long-player *The Dark Side of the Moon*, the looped clink-clank of the cash-register and coin sounds at the beginning of the cut lay out the song's unusual beat (in 5/4 time), and the rest of the recording is built on that.

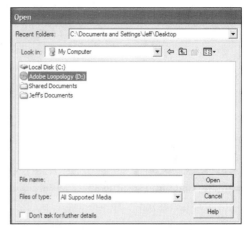

Figure 7.1 Open the *Loopology* CD.

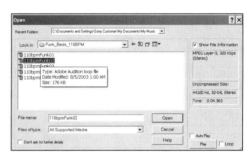

Figure 7.2 Access files and folders on the *Loopology* CD as you would any other CD content to import the sound files into Audition.

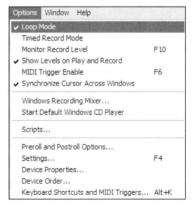

Figure 7.3 Select Loop Mode from the Options menu to preview the sound of your loop.

CREATING LOOPS

Making Precise Selections for Looping

If you want to use only the first bar, or four beats, of a loop, you need to select the part of the waveform that you want to use in your loop. You can do this directly within Edit view by dragging to select the portion of the waveform that you want to keep (**Figure 7.4**).

The problem with this approach is that it's hard to get exactly the selection you want, even if you're very careful where you click and drag. To accomplish this task with a bit more precision, choose Edit > Auto-Cue and select Find Beats and Mark (**Figure 7.5**).

Figure 7.4 The most obvious way to grab a portion of a waveform is the old click-and-drag approach, but it's not the most precise way to select the first bar of a sound clip before you loop it.

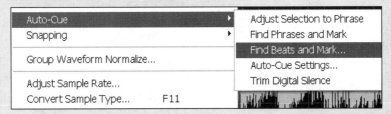

Figure 7.5 For a more precise approach, choose Auto-Cue > Find Beats and Mark from the Edit menu.

continues on next page

Making Precise Selections for Looping *(continued)*

A dialog box will appear, showing the Decibel Rise and Rise Time values (which Audition uses to define a beat). Once you have accepted or adjusted these values, click OK. Audition will create visual pointers in the waveform display to show you exactly where the individual beats are (**Figure 7.6**). Then you can simply count the number of beats you want to use in your loop and drag to select just that part of the sound file (**Figure 7.7**).

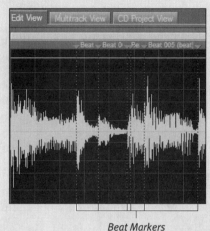

Figure 7.6
The Find Beats and Mark option makes it easier to make a selection specifying the portion of a file you want to loop.

Beat Markers

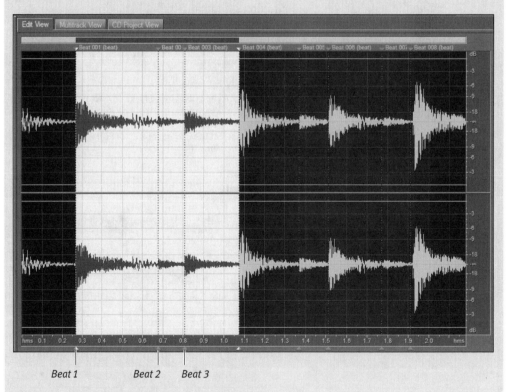

Beat 1 *Beat 2* *Beat 3*

Figure 7.7 This selection was made based on beat markers in the waveform.

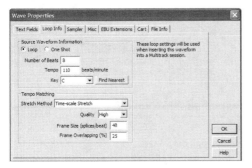

Figure 7.8 The Loop Info tab of the Wave Properties window is the control center for your loop.

Fine-Tuning Your Loop

Once you've created your loop, you can fine-tune its properties, which include tempo, key, and number of beats. To do this, you need to access the Loop Info tab of the Wave Properties window.

To adjust loop properties:

1. Open the Loop Info tab *by doing one of the following:*
   ▲ Choose View > Wave Properties (or press Ctrl+P).
   ▲ Right-click the waveform and select Wave Properties from the pop-up menu.
   The Loop Info tab opens (**Figure 7.8**).

2. Select the Loop button to activate loop playback for your file. Check the field that shows the number of beats in your file. If the number is incorrect, enter the correct number.

3. In the Key field, specify the musical key of your file. If you don't know the key, click Find Nearest and Audition will try to determine it for you.

✔ Tips

■ Entering the number of beats allows Audition to calculate the tempo. Audition's ability to detect beats is impressive, but you'll still want to double-check its work. If Audition seems to be getting it wrong, check to see that the settings in Edit > Find Beats > Beat Settings are configured properly to work with the kind of file you have open.

■ For a simple drum, percussion, or sound-effects file, select Non-Voiced. For files that contain chords, melodies, or other musical information, pick the appropriate key. Note that Find Nearest works best with simple, solo-instrument files.

■ Specifying a key creates a reference so that later, when you're working in Multitrack mode and want to use more than one loop at a time, Audition will know how to adjust the key of each file so that they play in the same key.

Setting Tempo Matching

The last step in tweaking your loop, and a very important one, is selecting a tempo-matching method. This lets Audition know how, if at all, you want your loop to conform to other loops and sounds with which you might match it in a session or multitrack environment. Five methods are available from the Stretch Method menu on the Loop Info panel (**Figure 7.9**).

Once you've adjusted the loop properties and selected your stretching method, you're all done! You have created your loop and it's ready for use in a multitrack composition.

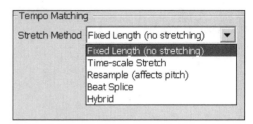

Figure 7.9 Tempo-matching options on the Stretch Method pull-down menu.

To choose a tempo-matching method:

◆ On the Loop Info panel, open the Stretch Method menu and *choose one of the following:*

▲ **Fixed Length (No Stretching):** Make this selection if you want the file to remain as is, exempt from any time stretching or pitch shifting. If you create a session with two or more fixed-length loops, they will not be adjusted to match each other in tempo or key.

▲ **Time-scale Stretch:** This setting tells Audition to stretch your file based on its actual duration rather than on beats, without affecting the pitch or key. This setting is recommended for synthesizer pads or other sustained background sounds that don't contain articulated beats.

▲ **Resample (Affects Pitch):** With
this method, Audition resamples
your file to stretch or compress its
duration, and the key also changes
accordingly. This is analogous to
speeding up or slowing down a
traditional tape recorder.

▲ **Beat Splice:** This option is best
used to speed up drum or percussion
tracks or any track that contains
a well-defined beat. To slow down
drum tracks, Adobe recommends
using Time-scale Stretch rather
than Beat Splice.

▲ **Hybrid:** Select this option to use
Time-scale Stretch settings when you
slow down your file, and Beat Splice
settings when you speed it up.

Using a Loop in a Multitrack Composition

When you've created your loop, the next step will likely be using it in a multitrack composition. Looped percussion tracks, in particular, make an ideal foundation upon which you can pile various other sounds and instruments. To begin, you need to move your new loop file from Edit View, where it was created and refined, into Multitrack view.

To move your loop into Multitrack view:

◆ With your loop file open, *do one of the following:*

▲ Choose Edit > Insert in Multitrack (or press Ctrl+M).

▲ Right-click the waveform and select Insert in Multitrack from the pop-up menu.

You'll see Audition's Multitrack view, and your loop file will be there, complete with loop icon (**Figure 7.10**). You can click the tab at the bottom right and drag your file across the display window to repeat the loop as many times as you wish.

✔ Tips

■ When you're working with multiple loops containing beats in Multitrack view, it's best to use the Bars and Beats display. This display measures time in bars, beats, and ticks, allowing you to sync beat information for multiple loops more easily. Right-click the meter at the bottom of the wave display, choose Display Time Format, and select Bars and Beats (**Figure 7.11**).

■ You can drag a loop fully or partially. If you extend a two-bar loop across five bars, for example, your loop will stop playing in the middle of its third repetition.

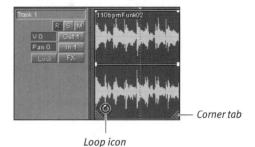

Corner tab

Loop icon

Figure 7.10 Once you've brought your loop file into Multitrack view, you can click the bottom-right Corner tab and drag your file across the display window to repeat it as many times as you wish.

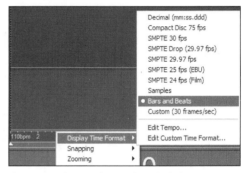

Figure 7.11 When working with multiple loops containing beats in Multitrack view, it's best to change the display setting to Bars and Beats to allow easier syncing of your loops.

Creating Your Own Percussion Loops

One of the most common uses for loops is to create a percussion track. For instance, if you've heard the song "Stupid Girl" by Garbage, you may recognize the looped drum beat; it's a sample from The Clash's 1979 recording "Train in Vain."

If you don't have the cash it takes to license a sample from an existing copyrighted recording, you can choose or create your own percussion samples to loop. You can find innumerable royalty-free samples on the Internet, which you can download for free. You can also buy CD-ROMs full of such files. And members of various online communities may be willing to trade some of their own original samples for some of yours.

If you want to create your own drum or percussion samples, here are a few tips:

- Find a high-quality source. If vinyl noise or digital artifacts are desirable to you, that's great, but if not, pay attention to the quality of the audio signal coming into your sound card.

- Find the most appropriate few seconds of a recording to sample. Look for a part where the drums are playing solo.

- Get into the habit of buying CD singles. Typically, these inexpensive modern-day equivalents of the vinyl 45 contain remixes of familiar songs, some of which may include interesting beats (*sans* other instruments).

- It depends on the source, but most drum beats will sound just as good in mono as they do in stereo. Whenever possible, convert a stereo source to mono; the resulting file will be smaller, and when you're mixing, you may appreciate the easier time you'll have working with a mono track.

USING A LOOP IN A MULTITRACK COMPOSITION

USING THE MULTITRACK VIEW

8

The Multitrack view in Audition is analogous to a virtual tape recorder, but with all the advantages of digital editing and processing. You can blend sounds and clips using up to 128 tracks. You can add effects nondestructively. You can edit and re-edit with ease, without razor blades and splice tape—and with the ability to undo your work if you're not pleased with the results. The possibilities are vast, and you're going to want to get to know the Multitrack view intimately if you're serious about multitrack recording and mixing.

A multitrack session consists of a series of tracks, each of which contains audio clips. In this chapter, I'll discuss sessions, tracks, and clips in detail and the various ways you can configure them. I'll also show how to bring MIDI files into a multitrack session, add real-time effects to your tracks, use buses to group tracks together, and change mix settings over time by using envelopes.

Multitrack View Features

Open the Multitrack view by selecting the Multitrack tab. Multitrack view (**Figure 8.1**) can look intimidating when you first see it, but it's well worth your time to get to know it. Its many tools and functions will prove invaluable to you as you start to mix tracks.

Audition's performance in multitrack projects depends heavily on the computer resources available to it. It's a good idea to keep your eye on how the program is using resources such as memory, processing power, and disk space. Two features of the Multitrack view environment, the mix gauge and load meter, can help you do that.

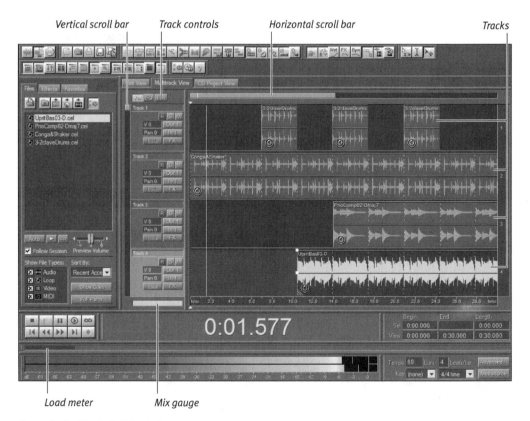

Figure 8.1 Audition's Multitrack view.

When you make a change to a track—moving an audio clip or changing its panning, EQ, or volume settings, for example—Audition starts a process called background mixing. When background mixing is complete, you can hear the changes you've made (which are, you may recall, nondestructive to the original audio files being used) during multi-track playback. The mix gauge shows you the progress of the background mixing process.

The load meter displays the amount of computer processor power available. You'll want to pay extra attention to this meter when using real-time effects, which can be quite demanding of processor power.

✔ Tips

■ You can disable or configure background mixing by right-clicking the mix gauge and selecting the appropriate item on the pop-up menu.

■ You can toggle between viewing and hiding the load meter by choosing Window > Load Meter.

MULTITRACK VIEW FEATURES

Configuring Multitrack Settings

To optimize Audition's performance on your computer while working on multitrack sessions, you can configure some settings on the Multitrack tab of the Options > Settings window (**Figure 8.2**).

◆ **Playback Buffer Size:** Determines the amount of audio, measured in seconds, that can be stored in a buffer during multitrack playback. Increasing this value can lighten the load on your computer's processor, while taking up more memory. For most sound cards, the default setting of a one-second buffer should suffice.

◆ **Playback Buffers:** Indicates how many buffers Audition can use during playback. The default setting is 10.

◆ **Recording Buffer Size:** Sets aside a memory buffer for use during multitrack recording. You may try increasing the default value of two seconds if your recordings contain dropouts (brief bursts of silence interrupting the audio).

◆ **Recording Buffers:** Indicates how many buffers Audition can use during recording. The default setting is 10.

◆ **Background Mixing Priority:** Indicates the priority of the background mixing process above or below other computer system events. The default setting is 2; the lower the number, the higher the priority. (You can use decimal values, such as 0.5.)

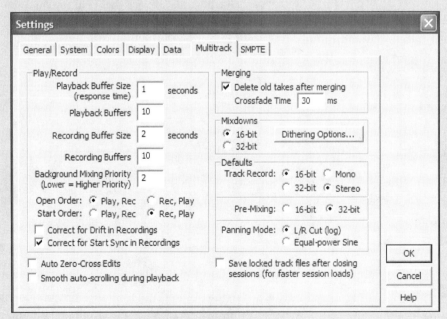

Figure 8.2 The Multitrack tab of the Options > Settings window.

continues on next page

MULTITRACK VIEW FEATURES

Configuring Multitrack Settings *(continued)*

◆ **Open Order** and **Start Order:** Specify the order in which Audition opens or starts a sound card's recording and playback ports. For most modern sound cards, these settings are obsolete.

◆ **Correct for Drift in Recordings:** Resamples recorded audio if it ends up mismatched with other tracks due to out-of-sync recording and playback devices.

◆ **Correct for Start Sync in Recordings:** Adjusts the start time of a newly recorded track if it does not match up with the start time of other tracks during playback.

◆ **Delete Old Takes After Merging:** Saves hard disk space by deleting unused takes after a punch-in.

◆ **Crossfade Time:** Determines the length in milliseconds of the crossfade that occurs when a punch-in is incorporated into the surrounding audio.

◆ **Mixdowns:** Determines the bit depth of a session mixdown. Click the Dithering Options button to enable and configure dithering.

◆ **Track Record:** Creates a default setting for recording in Multitrack view. You can choose 16- or 32-bit and mono or stereo.

◆ **Pre-mixing:** Determines the bit depth used for background mixing; the default is 32-bit.

◆ **Panning Mode:** Helps control volume changes during panning. Selecting L/R Cut (Log) enables panning to one side by lowering the volume of the other side; selecting Equal-Power Sine enables panning without any loss of volume.

◆ **Auto Zero-Cross Edits:** Enables automatic snapping of start and end points of cut, copied, and pasted audio to the closest zero-amplitude point, to avoid audible clicks at edit points.

◆ **Smooth Auto-Scrolling During Playback:** Enables smooth scrolling as opposed to paging-type scrolling, which is the default in Multitrack view. Leaving this option deselected will be less taxing on your computer's resources.

◆ **Save Locked Track Files After Closing Sessions:** Retains the temporary files created when tracks are locked, so that they can be reused when a session is reopened.

Working with Sessions

If you expect to use the same device property and master volume settings for most or all of your multitrack projects, you can save a session as a default after you've set it up the way you want it. This procedure allows you to use the default session as a template for future projects.

When you save a session, Audition stores it in .ses format. An .ses file does not actually contain audio. Storing a type of information called metadata, it functions as a kind of map, specifying what individual audio files to use, what portions of them to include, and where and how to use them.

To avoid headaches, try to save your session file and all the associated individual audio files in the same folder on your computer's hard drive. (When saving a session, you'll have the option of copying all associated audio files into the same directory on your computer. You might want to take advantage of this option if your files are scattered all over the place, but be careful if disk space is an issue for you.)

You can also insert time in a session, adding a specified amount of silence at a particular spot. This can be helpful if you plan to punch in audio later (see "Punching In and Choosing Takes" later in this chapter), or just want to leave room for an as-yet unspecified piece of audio.

To set a default session:

1. Choose File > Default Session > Set Current Session as Default (**Figure 8.3**).

2. If a Session Contains Clips window opens, click Yes (**Figure 8.4**).

   Audition saves your current session as the default session.

Figure 8.3 Set a current session as the default if you want to use the same device properties and volume settings in future sessions.

Figure 8.4 Audition checks to make sure you still want to set the default session, warning that the same clips may not be available in the future.

Figure 8.5 Use this File menu command to clear the Default Session setting.

✔ Tip

- You can remove the default session by choosing File > Default Session > Clear Default Session (**Figure 8.5**).

Figure 8.6 Choose File > New Session to start a new session.

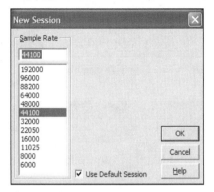

Figure 8.7 The New Session dialog box.

Figure 8.8 You can use this File menu command to save your session.

Save Session

Save Session As

Figure 8.9 The toolbar contains buttons for saving sessions.

To create a new session:

1. Choose File > New Session (**Figure 8.6**). The New Session window opens (**Figure 8.7**).

2. Select the sample rate you want to use.

3. Click the Use Default Session button if you want to use the device assignments and master volume settings specified in your default session.

4. Click OK.

   A new session opens.

✔ Tip

■ If you haven't set a default session, the Use Default Session check box will not appear in the New Session window.

To save a session:

1. *Do one of the following:*

   ▲ To save changes to the open session file, choose File > Save Session (**Figure 8.8**), or click the Save Session button on the toolbar (**Figure 8.9**).

   ▲ To save changes to a new session file, choose File > Save Session As, or click the Save Session As button on the toolbar.

   ▲ To save changes to all open sessions, choose File > Save All.

continues on next page

2. In the Save Session or Save Session As dialog box (**Figure 8.10**), browse to the folder in which you want to save your session; in the File Name field, give the session a name.

3. If you want to copy all audio files used in your session to the same directory, select the Save Copies of All Associated Files check box.

4. Click Save.

Audition saves the session in the directory you selected.

✔ Tips

■ After you select the Save Copies of All Associated Files option, click the Options button to open the Session 'Save Copies of all files' Options window (**Figure 8.11**). There, you can convert those files to a different format or sampling rate.

■ If you change the sampling rate, you can enable and configure dithering by clicking the Conversion Properties button (for more on dithering, see Chapter 2).

To insert time in a session:

1. Click the point in the session timeline where you want the inserted time to begin.

2. Choose Edit > Insert/Delete Time.

The Insert/Delete Time window opens.

3. Select Insert and enter the amount of time you want to insert in the Decimal Time field (**Figure 8.12**).

4. Click OK.

The program inserts a new, blank space in the session of the length you specified, starting at the point you clicked. Audio to the right of that point is shifted to the right to make room for the added time.

Figure 8.10 The Save Session As dialog box.

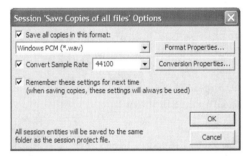

Figure 8.11 The Session 'Save copies of all files' Options dialog box.

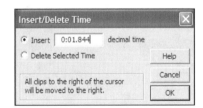

Figure 8.12 Specify the amount of time you want to insert in a session.

Figure 8.13 Clip tools on the toolbar.

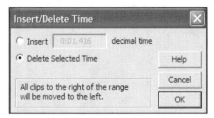

Figure 8.14 Select Delete Selected Time to remove a selection from a session.

To delete time in a session:

1. Click either the Time Selection or Hybrid Tool toolbar button (**Figure 8.13**).

2. Select the audio in the session that you want to delete.

3. Choose Edit > Insert/Delete Time. The Insert/Delete Time window opens.

4. Select Delete Selected Time (**Figure 8.14**). Note that if you haven't made a selection first, this button will be dimmed.

5. Click OK. The program deletes the selection, moving audio to the right of the selection to the left, to prevent a gap in the session.

✔ Tip

■ You must unlock any locked tracks in a session before inserting or deleting time. (See "Adding Real-Time Effects" later in this chapter for information on locked tracks.)

WORKING WITH SESSIONS

Configuring Session Properties

If it's not already visible, you can view the Session Properties window in the Multitrack view work area (**Figure 8.15**) by choosing Window > Session Properties. In this window, you can specify the tempo, key, time signature, and beats per bar for the loop files in your current session. The loop files will conform to these settings (other files will not change).

Figure 8.15 The Session Properties window.

The Advanced button brings up the Advanced Session Properties window, which you can also access by choosing View > Advanced Session Properties. This window contains five tabs:

1. **General**: You can specify a time within a session at which playback will always begin. You can also select a musical key to which looped files will conform.

2. **Mixing**: You can specify a bit depth for background mixing, a panning method for stereo waveforms, a preferred place for the Master Volume slider when using a Bus FX, and a volume envelope range. (Bus FXs and envelopes are covered later in this chapter.)

3. **Tempo**: You can specify various tempo settings and see (and manipulate) the current cursor position in bars-and-beats format.

4. **Metronome**: You can enable a metronome, which will click to keep time during session playback. You can choose a particular sound, a volume level, a time signature, and a playback device for the metronome.

5. **Notes**: You can enter information about your session, for your own (or others') future reference.

Configuring Tracks

In terms of track availability, Audition leaves your four-track cassette "portastudio" in the dust. You can record and mix up to 128 tracks in a session.

There is a track-controls area to the left of each track's waveform in the Display window. You can click the Vol, EQ, and Bus buttons to toggle among different track properties settings. However, you may prefer to configure all the available track properties in one place. You can access them all in the Track Properties window.

To configure tracks in the Track Properties window:

1. *Do one of the following:*

▲ In the Multitrack view Display pane, select the track you want to configure and then choose Window > Track Properties.

▲ In the Display pane, right-click the track-controls area (but not in a field) for the track you want to configure.

The Track Properties window opens (**Figure 8.16**).

2. Configure the options.

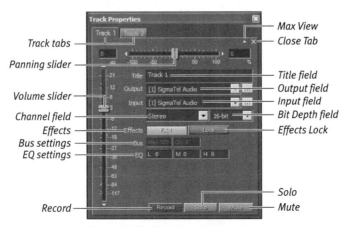

Track tabs

Panning slider

Volume slider

Channel field

Effects

Bus settings

EQ settings

Record

Max View

Close Tab

Title field

Output field

Input field

Bit Depth field

Effects Lock

Solo

Mute

Figure 8.16 The Track Properties window.

continues on next page

CONFIGURING TRACKS

✔ Tips

- In the Vol and EQ track-controls areas, you can right-click the volume and panning fields to access sliders (**Figure 8.17**).

- Widen the track-control area to add more functionality. Just click the line that divides it from the waveform displays and drag it to the right. If you do this with the Vol button selected in the track controls, for example, you can access high, middle, and low EQ controls as well as the standard volume controls (**Figure 8.18**).

- Choose Window > Mixer for an alternate way of viewing, tweaking, and mixing tracks. The Track Mixer tab does not give you all the functionality of the track display, but it can make viewing and configuring many tracks at once easier.

Figure 8.17 You can right-click the volume and panning fields in the Track Properties window to access slider controls.

Figure 8.18 Widening the Volume track-controls area reveals EQ settings.

Track Properties Window Settings

The Track Properties window makes it easy to fiddle with all of a track's configuration settings in one place. It's generally more user-friendly than the track-controls area next to the track display, which can be rather cramped. The configuration tools include the following:

- **Track tabs:** Use these tabs to access properties of different tracks. These appear only after you've opened the Track Properties windows of more than one track (Figure 8.16).

- **Max View button:** Click to hide the track tabs and provide more room in the window. Click again to restore the tabs.

- **Close tab:** Click to close the open tab.

- **Volume slider:** Move the slider up or down to adjust the volume. You can also specify a volume value in decibels in the field above the slider.

- **Panning slider:** Move the slider left or right to pan the track in the stereo field. You can also specify a panning percentage in the field next to the slider (positive percentages pan to the right, negative ones to the left).

continues on next page

CONFIGURING TRACKS

Track Properties Window Settings *(continued)*

◆ **Title:** Enter a name for the track if you don't want to use the generic Track 1, Track 2, and so on.

◆ **Output** and **Input:** Use these fields to specify the devices you want to use for recording and playback in this track.

◆ **Channel field:** Choose Left Only, Right Only, or Stereo to specify what part of a stereo waveform you want to use in the track.

◆ **Bit Depth field:** Use this field to select the track's bit depth.

◆ **FX:** Click to show the Effects Rack (**Figure 8.19**) for the track.

◆ **Lock:** Click to lock or unlock real-time effects settings for the track.

◆ **Bus:** Drag across these fields to change the wet and dry values for the track if it's used in a bus.

◆ **EQ:** Drag across these fields to manipulate low, middle, and high EQ settings.

◆ **Record button:** Click to enable the track for recording.

◆ **Solo button:** Click if you want to hear this track by itself during playback. (Hold down Ctrl while clicking the Solo buttons of multiple tracks if you want to isolate a particular combination of tracks during playback.)

◆ **Mute button:** Click to mute this track during playback.

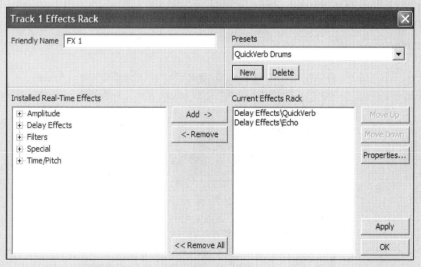

Figure 8.19 Use the Effects Rack to add effects to a track.

CONFIGURING TRACKS

Equalizing Tracks

Not all audio sounds perfect in its natural form, and you may need to equalize your tracks to compensate for imperfections. For example, a little high-end boost can brighten dull signals, and tweaking the mid-range of a vocal track can help it stand out in a dense mix.

You can use the track-controls area to tweak basic EQ settings, but at times you may want to open a full-featured, one-stop window for equalization.

To equalize tracks in the Track Equalizers window:

1. *Do one of the following:*

   ▲ In the Multitrack view Display window, select the track that you want to equalize and then choose Window > Track EQ.

   ▲ In the EQ track-controls area of the track that you want to equalize, right-click the H, M, or L EQ field.

   The Track Equalizers window opens (**Figure 8.20**).

2. Configure the options.

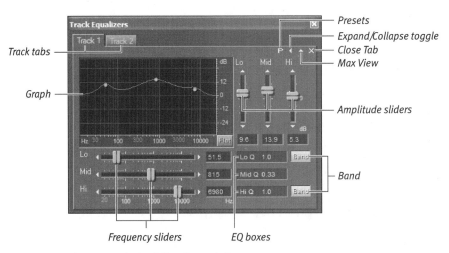

Figure 8.20 The Track Equalizers window.

EQUALIZING TRACKS

Track Equalizers Window Settings

◆ **Track tabs:** Use these tabs to select a track to equalize. These tabs appear only after you've opened the Track Equalizers windows of more than one track.

Figure 8.21 The EQ Presets window.

◆ **Presets button:** Click to open the EQ Presets window (**Figure 8.21**), where you can save your current settings as a preset for subsequent use, or delete existing presets.

◆ **Max View button:** Click to hide the track tabs and provide more room in the window. Click again to restore the tabs.

◆ **Expand/Collapse button:** Click to expand the graph display, at the expense of the frequency, amplitude, and Q sliders and text boxes. Click again to switch back.

◆ **Close tab:** Click to close the open tab.

◆ **Graph:** This graph represents your EQ settings visually. The *x*-axis shows frequency, and the *y*-axis shows amplitude. Instead of using the other controls, you can drag the control points around the graph to manipulate the EQ.

◆ **Q boxes:** These boxes display the high-, mid-, and low-frequency Q (frequency bandwidth) values. To change these values, click the box and drag to the right or left.

◆ **Band buttons:** Click to enable the high- and low-frequency Q boxes.

◆ **Frequency sliders:** Move these sliders to the left or right to decrease or increase frequency values (your changes will be reflected in the graph as you do). You can also specify Hz values in the fields to the right of the sliders.

◆ **Amplitude sliders:** Move these sliders up or down to increase or decrease frequency amplitude. You can also specify dB values in the fields beneath the sliders.

EQUALIZING TRACKS

Using Clips

In the context of multitrack audio in Audition, you can think of a clip as a piece of audio that exists within a track.

It's easy to select clips and move them or align them with each other. You can even split clips into smaller clips, and you can reconnect them later if you like. You can time-stretch a clip to change its length without affecting pitch. You can insert an empty audio clip into a track or session as a placeholder. To make it easier to identify and manipulate more than one clip at a time, you can create clip groups. For example, you can create a group of clips that contains all the percussion parts in a session. Clips in a group appear in a different color and with a clip group icon.

To configure clip properties:

1. Right-click the clip you want to configure and choose Audio Clip Properties (**Figure 8.22**).

   The Audio Clip Properties window opens (**Figure 8.23**).

2. Configure the settings.

✔ Tip

- You can use sliders or numeric value fields in the Audio Clip Properties window to control the clip's volume, panning, and even color. You can also choose to mute the clip or to lock the clip so that it can't be moved.

Figure 8.22 Right-click a clip to select Audio Clip Properties.

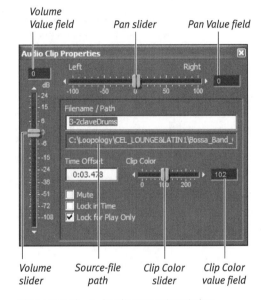

Figure 8.23 The Audio Clip Properties window.

Selected clip

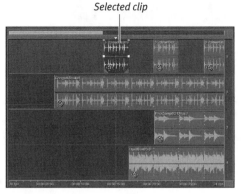

Figure 8.24 Click a clip in the track display to select it.

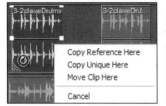

Figure 8.25
When you copy a clip to another location, you'll need to select an option in this menu.

To move clips:

1. *Do one of the following:*
   - ▲ To move a single clip, click the clip (**Figure 8.24**).
   - ▲ To move all clips on a track, click the track and then choose Edit > Select All Clips in [Track Name].
   - ▲ To move all clips in the session, choose Edit > Select All Clips.

2. On the toolbar, click the Move/Copy Clip tool.

3. Drag the selected clips.

✔ Tip

- ■ You can use the Hybrid tool instead of the Move/Copy Clip tool to move clips. If you do, you must right-click the clips before you drag them.

To copy a clip:

1. On the toolbar, click the Move/Copy Clip tool.

2. Right-click the clip and drag it to the location where you want to place the new copy.

3. Release the mouse button to drop the clip. A pop-up menu appears (**Figure 8.25**).

4. From the menu, *select one of the following:*
   - ▲ **Copy Reference Here:** Makes a copy that uses the same original audio file as the original clip, so that any edits you make to the original audio file will be reflected in both clips.
   - ▲ **Copy Unique Here:** Makes a copy that uses its own version of the audio file that the original clip uses, which you can then edit without affecting the original clip.
   - ▲ **Move Clip Here:** Moves, rather than creates a new copy of, the selected clip.

continues on next page

USING CLIPS

✔ Tips

- Instead of copying a clip, you can select a clip and choose Edit > Clip Duplicate. In the Clip Duplicate window (**Figure 8.26**), you can choose to repeat the clip in a track with no gaps or with gaps of a certain length. This approach is a good way to reproduce a clip many times without consuming additional disk space.

- If you are copying a MIDI clip, the Copy Unique Here option will not be available.

To align clips:

1. Hold down the Ctrl key while you click the clips that you want to align.

2. *Do one of the following:*
   - ▲ To give all the selected clips the same start point, choose Edit > Align Left, or right-click one of the clips and choose Align Left.
   - ▲ To give all the selected clips the same end point, choose Edit > Align Right, or right-click one of the clips and choose Align Right.

To split a clip:

1. On the toolbar, click either the Time Selection tool or the Hybrid tool.

2. *Do one of the following:*
   - ▲ To split a clip into two pieces, click the waveform where you want the split located.
   - ▲ To split a clip into three pieces, click the waveform to create one cut point and then drag until you reach the second desired cut point.

3. On the toolbar, click the Split Clip button (**Figure 8.27**).

   The clip is split into either two or three smaller clips.

Figure 8.26 The Clip Duplicate window.

Split Clip

Figure 8.27 Enable the Split Clip button to cut a clip into smaller pieces.

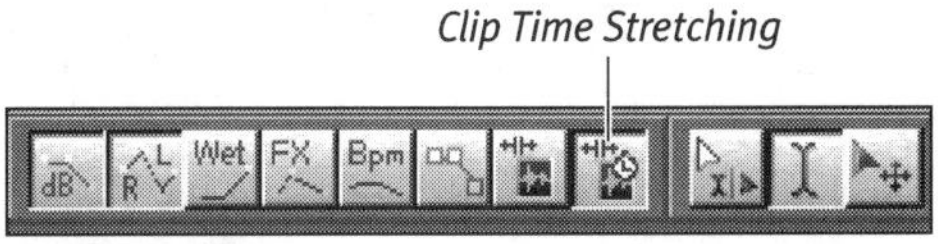

Clip Time Stretching

Figure 8.28 Enable the Clip Time Stretching button to change a clip's length without altering its pitch.

Figure 8.29 The Clip Time Stretch Properties window.

Figure 8.30 The Insert > Empty Audio Clip menu.

To rejoin split clips:

1. On the toolbar, click either the Move/Copy Clip tool or the Hybrid tool.

2. Make sure the clips to be rejoined are lined up next to each other in the same track.

3. Right-click one of the clips and select Merge/Rejoin Split in the pop-up menu.

To time-stretch a clip:

1. On the toolbar, click the Clip Time Stretching button (**Figure 8.28**).

2. Select the clip you want to time-stretch.

3. Click either bottom corner of the clip and drag in the appropriate direction to change the length of the clip.

✔ Tip

■ Right-click the clip and select Clip Time Stretch Properties. In the window that opens (**Figure 8.29**), you can choose from the four different time-stretching methods available in Audition (see Chapter 7).

To insert an empty audio clip:

1. In the Display window, make a selection where you want to insert the clip (the length of your selection will determine the length of the empty clip).

2. Choose Insert > Empty Audio Clip (**Figure 8.30**) and *select one of the following*:

   ▲ **In Current Track (Stereo):** Places an empty stereo clip in the currently selected track.

   ▲ **In Current Track (Mono):** Places an empty mono clip in the currently selected track.

   ▲ **In All Record-Armed Tracks:** Places empty clips in every track that's currently record-enabled via the R button in the track-controls area.

To crossfade a pair of clips:

1. Make sure the clips to be crossfaded are on separate tracks.

2. Move the clips so that the end of one overlaps the beginning of the other.

3. Make a selection in the overlapping area where you want the crossfade to occur.

4. Hold down the Ctrl key while you click both clips.

5. Choose Edit > Crossfade (**Figure 8.31**) and choose the type of crossfade you want:

   ▲ **Linear:** Produces a crossfade with even fades (**Figure 8.32**).

   ▲ **Sinusoidal:** Produces a crossfade with a more curved slope (**Figure 8.33**).

   ▲ **Logarithmic In:** Produces a crossfade in which one sound fades out quickly and steeply, and the other sound fades in at a slower, steadier rate (**Figure 8.34**).

   ▲ **Logarithmic Out:** Produces a crossfade in which one sound fades in quickly and steeply, and the other sound fades out at a slower, steadier rate (**Figure 8.35**).

Figure 8.31 The Edit > Crossfade menu offers four types of crossfades.

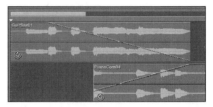

Figure 8.32 A linear crossfade.

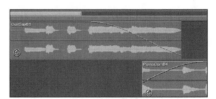

Figure 8.33 A sinusoidal crossfade.

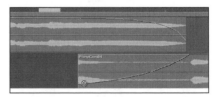

Figure 8.34 A logarithmic-in crossfade.

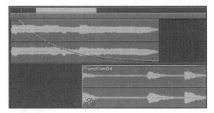

Figure 8.35 A logarithmic-out crossfade.

USING CLIPS

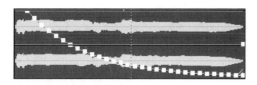

Figure 8.36 Clicking a crossfade line in the track display reveals control points.

Clip Group icons

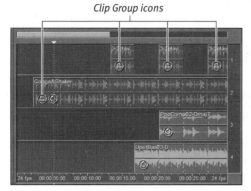

Figure 8.37 When a clip group is created, a new icon appears on each clip in the group.

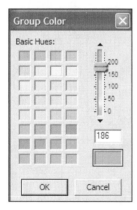

Figure 8.38 Choose your own color for a clip group in the Group Color window.

✔ Tip

- Once you've created a crossfade, you can click the resulting line or curve in the waveform to access control points (**Figure 8.36**). You can drag these control points to fine-tune the crossfade.

To create a clip group:

1. Hold down the Ctrl key while you click the clips you want to include in the group.

2. *Do one of the following:*
   - ▲ Choose Edit > Group Clips.
   - ▲ Right-click any of the selected clips and choose Group Clips from the pop-up menu.

   A clip group is created, the color of the grouped clips changes, and clip group icon appears on each clip (**Figure 8.37**).

✔ Tips

- You can ungroup a clip group by selecting any clip in the group and choosing Edit > Group Clips again or by right-clicking any clip in the group and deselecting Group Clips.

- You can change a clip group's color by choosing Edit > Group Color or by right-clicking a clip in the group and selecting Group Color. You can pick a color in the Group Color window (**Figure 8.38**).

To remove a clip from a session:

1. Select the clips you want to remove.

2. *Do one of the following:*
   - ▲ To remove clips from the track display while keeping the associated audio files open and available in the Organizer window, Insert menu, and Edit view, choose Edit > Remove Clips.
   - ▲ To remove clips from the track display and close the associated audio files, choose Edit > Destroy Clips.

USING CLIPS

Multitrack Snapping Options

When working with loops and other clips in a multitrack session, you may have an easier time moving clips if you enable snapping.

In the Multitrack view, choose Edit > Snapping (**Figure 8.39**) to enable snapping. There are two multitrack-specific options you may want to enable:

◆ **Snap to Clips:** Snaps clips to the beginning or end of other clips.

◆ **Snap to Loop Endpoints:** Snaps clips to the beginning or end of loops.

Figure 8.39 Choose Edit › Snapping to enable snapping, which can provide smoother-sounding results when you move clips.

Punching In and Choosing Takes

Let's say you've just recorded a vocal track in a session, and it sounds great except for just one muffed line. You can replace that line by punching in, or re-recording just that line without affecting the rest of the track. It's been a common practice in conventional recording studios for decades (you don't really believe Jimi Hendrix played *every* solo perfectly the first time, do you?), and it's easier than ever in a digital recording environment.

In Audition, punching in is a simple matter of selecting the audio you want to replace in the track display, right-clicking it, and choosing Punch In. Then, when you hit the record button, you simply re-record your part. There's no need to hit the stop button when you're done; when punching in, the recording stops automatically at the end of the selected audio segment.

If you want to stockpile several takes of your punch-in and then pick the best one later, right-click on the selection and choose Allow Multiple Takes before punching in. Then you can punch in multiple times, and each take will be saved (you'll see them pile up in the Organizer window). You can choose the one you want to use later.

You can listen to individual takes by right-clicking the clip and selecting a take in the Take History submenu. The same submenu also contains options for deleting a selected take, or merging one into the track (when you've identified the one you want to use).

Figure 8.40 Right-click a track and choose Insert › MIDI to bring a MIDI file into a multitrack session.

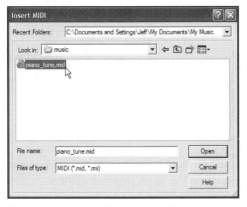

Figure 8.41 Browse to find the MIDI clip you want to use.

Importing MIDI Files

You can easily bring a MIDI file into a multi-track session. Once you have, you can fine-tune its volume, tempo, key, the instruments you hear on playback, and more.

To bring a MIDI clip into a track:

1. *Do one of the following:*
   - ▲ Right-click an empty track and choose Insert > MIDI from the pop-up menu (**Figure 8.40**).
   - ▲ Click an empty track and from the File menu choose Insert > MIDI.

2. Browse to and select a MIDI file on your computer (**Figure 8.41**).

3. Click Open.

   The MIDI file is inserted into the selected track.

continues on next page

✔ Tips

- After you've inserted a MIDI clip, a Map button appears in the track-controls area (**Figure 8.42**). This opens the MIDI Device Assignment window (**Figure 8.43**), where you can assign virtual MIDI instruments to playback devices, and the MIDI track itself to a specific MIDI channel in your setup.

- To play only one instrument in a MIDI clip, right-click the clip (or go to the Edit menu), choose Active Track, and choose the instrument in the submenu (**Figure 8.44**).

To adjust the volume of a MIDI clip:

1. Right-click the MIDI clip and select Set Controller 7.

    The MIDI Controller 7 (Volume) window opens (**Figure 8.45**).

2. In the Default Controller 7 box, enter a value for the volume.

3. Click OK.

    The volume of the MIDI clip is adjusted accordingly.

✔ Tip

- You can also change the key or tempo of a MIDI clip by using the Transpose and Set Tempo commands, located on both the Edit menu and the pop-up menu that appears when you right-click a MIDI clip.

Figure 8.42 A Map button appears in the track-controls area when a MIDI file is inserted in a track.

Figure 8.43 The MIDI Device Assignment window.

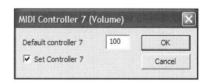

Figure 8.44 The Active Track menu allows you to play just one instrument in a MIDI clip.

Figure 8.45 The MIDI Controller 7 (Volume) window, which you can use to control the volume of a MIDI clip.

Figure 8.46 The Effects tab in the Organizer window.

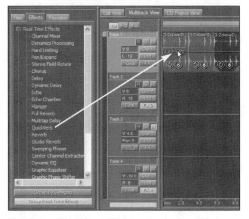

Figure 8.47 To add an effect to a track, drag it from the Organizer window to the appropriate track in the track display.

Figure 8.48 When you add an effect to a track, a corresponding effect configuration window opens.

Adding Real-Time Effects

A real-time effect is one that is added to audio nondestructively and that responds immediately to your tweaking. You can adjust the settings for a real-time effect as you're listening to a mix and hear the results in real time (or close to real time, depending on the speed and performance of your computer). Because the effect is nondestructive, you can easily remove it as well.

Adding an effect to a sound in a multitrack session is a simple drag-and-drop maneuver. In this example, you'll see how to add the QuickVerb effect to a drum clip in Track 1.

To add a real-time effect to a track:

1. Open the Effects tab in the Organizer window (**Figure 8.46**).

2. Locate the QuickVerb effect and drag it to Track 1 in the track display (**Figure 8.47**).

   The QuickVerb configuration tab opens (**Figure 8.48**).

✔ Tips

- Once an effect has been added, you can reconfigure it by clicking the FX button in the track-controls area.

- Right-click the FX button and choose Rack Setup to remove or reorder a track's effects or to create or apply effect presets.

To mix real-time effects:

1. Right-click a track's FX button and choose FX Mixer.

   The FX Mixer tab opens (**Figure 8.49**).

2. *Do any of the following:*

   ▲ To adjust the original signal's volume in relation to the effects being added to it, move the Dry Out slider up or down.

   ▲ To adjust each effect's volume in relation to the original signal and the other effects, move the effects sliders up or down.

   ▲ To mute an effect, click the effect's Bypass button.

3. *Do one of the following:*

   ▲ If you want an effect's input to receive the output from the previous effect, click the Serial button.

   ▲ If you want an effect's input to receive the output of the dry, original signal, click the Parallel button.

✔ Tips

■ When you choose the Serial option for an effect, you may notice that the Src (original signal) and Prv (output from the previous effect) field values are set to 0 and 100, respectively. When you choose the Parallel option, these settings are reversed. However, you can create your own Serial/Parallel hybrid settings by dragging across these fields to fine-tune the mix of dry signal and previous effect that the effect you're configuring receives.

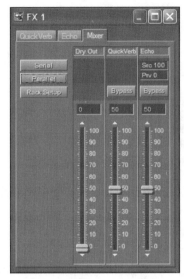

Figure 8.49 The FX Mixer window.

- Once you're satisfied with the effects you've added to a track, click the Lock button in the track-controls area to lock your settings in place and lighten the load on your computer processor. (Locked tracks are moved to the background mix and cannot be processed until they are unlocked.)

- To turn off all of a track's effects, right-click the FX button and select Bypass.

Using Audition as a ReWire Host

ReWire is a technology developed by Propellerhead Software that allows you to synchronize more than one audio application. Adobe Audition 1.5 can serve as a ReWire *host*, meaning that it can accept audio sent by another ReWire-capable application, or *slave*. You can enable ReWire hosting in Audition by using the ReWire tab in the Options > Device Properties window (**Figure 8.50**).

Once Audition has been configured as a ReWire host, you can assign input generated by ReWire slaves to tracks and configure it in an Audition multitrack project. You can convert a ReWire track to a normal audio track in Audition by right-clicking it in the track display and choosing Bounce.

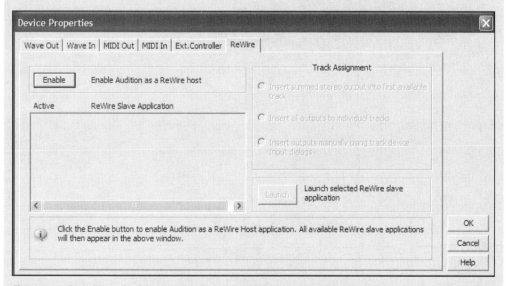

Figure 8.50 The ReWire tab of the Options > Device Properties window; click the Enable button to enable Audition as a ReWire host.

ADDING REAL-TIME EFFECTS

Using Buses

A bus allows you to manipulate several tracks at once, as if they were one individual track. Applying a real-time effect to a bus in one shot is significantly easier on your computer's resources than applying the same effect to the tracks individually. You can create up to 26 buses.

To create a bus:

1. Choose Window > Mixers.

2. Click the Bus Mixer tab.

   The Bus Mixer tab of the Mixers window opens (**Figure 8.51**).

3. Click the New button.

   The Bus Properties dialog box opens (**Figure 8.52**).

4. Choose an output device for the bus and, if you wish, a name.

5. In the Installed Real-Time Effects pane, select effects you want available for your bus and click Add to move them to the Current Effects Rack pane.

6. Click OK.

   The bus appears on the Bus Mixer tab of the Mixers window.

Figure 8.51 The Bus Mixer tab.

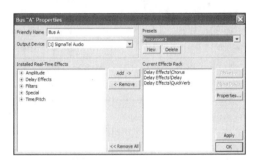

Figure 8.52 The Bus Properties dialog box.

To configure an existing bus:

1. Open the Bus Mixer tab in the Mixers window.

2. *Do one of the following:*

   To reconfigure the Bus Properties dialog box, click the Out button.

   To configure the effects you've chosen for this bus, click the Config button.

   Each effect has its own tab in the configuration window and its own controls.

To adjust bus panning:

◆ In the Bus Mixer tab, *do one of the following:*

   ▲ Move the small asterisk above the Pan field to one of three panning positions: hard left, center, or hard right.

   ▲ Drag in the Pan field below the asterisk to fine-tune the panning.

◆ Move the bus faders up or down to control the volume of the bus in a mix.

Mixing with Clip Envelopes

Clip envelopes allow you to change the volume, panning, and effects settings of a clip over the course of a mix.

To show or hide a line representing a particular envelope in a track's waveform, click the relevant button on the toolbar (**Figure 8.53**). Once an envelope line appears in the track display, you can enable the Edit Envelopes button to edit it.

To edit a clip envelope:

1. On the toolbar, click the Edit Envelopes button.

2. Select the clip in which you want to edit an envelope.

   Control points become visible along the envelope line of the clip (**Figure 8.54**).

3. *Do one of the following:*

   ▲ To manipulate the clip envelope, drag the control points. As you do, the values you're changing will appear next to your mouse pointer (**Figure 8.55**).

   ▲ To add a new control point, click anywhere along the envelope.

   ▲ To remove a control point, drag it off the clip.

   ▲ To clear all control points from a clip, right-click the clip and choose Envelopes in the pop-up menu. In the appropriate submenu (Volume, Pan, or FX Mix), choose Clear Selected Points.

   ▲ To change the envelope lines to spline curves (for smoother transitions), right-click the clip and choose Envelopes. In the appropriate submenu, choose Use Splines.

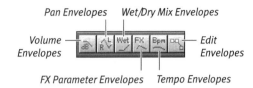

Figure 8.53 Toolbar buttons for showing or hiding clip envelopes.

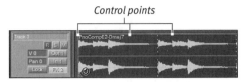

Figure 8.54 When the Edit Envelopes button is enabled, you can select a clip and see its envelope control points.

Figure 8.55 As you use the control points to manipulate envelopes, Audition shows the resulting changes in value.

✔ Tip

■ Note that tempo envelopes, which show the tempo of MIDI clips only, can be displayed but not edited.

MIXING WITH CLIP ENVELOPES

MULTICHANNEL AUDIO

9

The ability to create and export multichannel audio mixes helps make Audition a worthy addition to the Adobe Video Collection. Many people enjoy surround-sound home-theater setups today, thanks to the ability of DVDs and television broadcasts to deliver 5.1 audio. Any modern professional video project would suffer without the ability to work with multichannel audio. In many video projects, Audition's multichannel capabilities are sure to be useful.

But multichannel audio isn't just for video. During the past few years, DVD-Audio and Super Audio CD (SACD) have emerged as niche audio technologies, prized in audio-phile circles for delivering higher resolution than ordinary compact discs in addition to multichannel audio.

In this chapter, I'll explain how Audition can help you create and use multichannel audio. I'll show how the Multichannel Encoder can help you select, pan, and otherwise fine-tune tracks in a multichannel mix. I'll also discuss the options available for exporting multi-channel audio files.

5.1 Surround Sound

Audition supports 5.1 surround sound, which actually refers to six-channel audio. A 5.1 setup includes two speakers in the front (similar to traditional stereo speakers), with a third center channel between them and two more speakers in the rear. The extra ".1" is a low-frequency subwoofer for deep, pounding bass.

To preview a multichannel mix, you need a sound card with six outputs, set up as follows:

◆ **Output 1:** Left front speaker

◆ **Output 2:** Right front speaker

◆ **Output 3:** Center front speaker

◆ **Output 4:** Subwoofer

◆ **Output 5:** Left rear speaker

◆ **Output 6:** Right rear speaker

You must also have Microsoft DirectX 8.0 or later installed on your computer. Most likely, you installed DirectX during the Audition installation (it's one of the default options), but you may want to check Microsoft's Web site for any updates or patches.

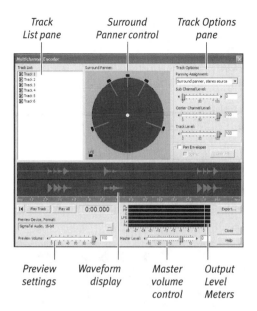

Track List pane *Surround Panner control* *Track Options pane*

Preview settings *Waveform display* *Master volume control* *Output Level Meters*

Figure 9.1 The Multichannel Encoder window contains all the tools you need to select, pan, and adjust the volume of tracks in your multichannel project and to preview and save your work.

Using the Multichannel Encoder

If you want to work with surround sound, you'll need to get to know Audition's Multichannel Encoder. There, you can specify which tracks you want to use in your multichannel mix, where they should appear in the audio field, how loud they should be, and how you would like to save your mix.

First, we'll take a quick look at the whole process. In the pages that follow, we'll examine the major steps and settings more closely.

To export multichannel audio using the Multichannel Encoder:

1. Create a session in Multitrack view, or open an existing one.

2. Adjust track volumes, stereo panning, and effects to your liking.

3. Choose View > Multichannel Encoder (Ctrl+E).

   The Multichannel Encoder window opens (**Figure 9.1**).

4. Click a track or bus in the Track List pane and configure the panning and level settings for it in the Track Options pane. Repeat this step for each track.

5. If desired, click Play All or Play Track to hear a preview of your audio.

6. Click Export to save your multichannel audio.

   Audition opens the Multichannel Export Options dialog box (see "Saving Multichannel Audio" later in this chapter).

✔ Tip

■ Make sure the tracks (and buses, if applicable) that you want to use in your multichannel mix are checked in the Track List pane before you configure the Track Options settings.

Tracks and Buses

If you've assigned one or more of the tracks in a multitrack project to a bus, you'll see the bus listed in the Track List pane of the Multichannel Encoder (**Figure 9.2**). Once it's in the Track List pane, you can pan and adjust the volume of the bus in your multichannel mix just as you would any individual track.

Sometimes you may want to use both the bus and the individual "dry" (without effects) tracks assigned to the bus in the same mix. To do so, you need to configure the Dry value in the Multitrack view.

To make a track assigned to a bus available in the Track List pane:

1. In Multitrack view, select the individual track that you want to have available in the Multichannel Encoder.

2. Click the Bus tab (**Figure 9.3**).

3. Click the Dry field and drag to the right to increase the value to a number above 0 (**Figure 9.4**).

4. Open the Multichannel Encoder.

   Both the bus and the individual track should be available in the Track List pane (Figure 9.2).

Figure 9.2 In the Track List pane, you can select tracks and buses for use in your multichannel mix.

Figure 9.3 The Bus tab.

Figure 9.4 For a bus to be available in the Multichannel Encoder, its Dry setting in the Multitrack View must be greater than 0.

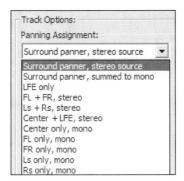

Figure 9.5 The Panning Assignment drop-down menu in the Track Options pane.

Setting the Panning Assignment

In the Panning Assignment menu in the Track Options pane (**Figure 9.5**), you can choose to use the Surround Panner to place a mono or stereo track in a particular location in the surround-sound field. You can also assign tracks to any of the individual channels, including the subwoofer.

To choose a Panning Assignment:

1. Choose View > Multichannel Encoder (Ctrl+E) to open the Multichannel Encoder window.

2. Click the Panning Assignment pull-down menu to reveal the Panning Assignment menu options:

   ▲ **Surround Panner, Stereo Source:** Allows you to use the Surround Panner to place a stereo source in any desired location in the surround-sound field. Left- and right-channel information will always be sent to the appropriate front and rear channels to preserve the separation of the original stereo track; the center channel will receive a summed combination of the two.

   ▲ **Surround Panner, Summed to Mono:** Sends a summed mono version of your track to all channels.

   ▲ **LFE Only:** Sends the selected track to the subwoofer channel.

   ▲ **FL + FR, Stereo:** Sends the selected track in stereo to the front left and right speakers.

   ▲ **Ls + Rs, Stereo:** Sends the selected track in stereo to the rear left and right speakers.

continues on next page

SETTING THE PANNING ASSIGNMENT

- ▲ **Center + LFE, Stereo:** Sends the left channel of a stereo track to the center speaker, and the right channel to the subwoofer. If the track is mono, both speakers will receive the same signal.
- ▲ **Center Only, Mono:** Sends the selected track in mono to the center channel.
- ▲ **FL Only, Mono:** Sends the selected track in mono to the front left channel.
- ▲ **FR Only, Mono:** Sends the selected track in mono to the front right channel.
- ▲ **Ls Only, Mono:** Sends the selected track in mono to the rear left channel.
- ▲ **Rs Only, Mono:** Sends the selected track in mono to the rear right channel.

3. Select a Panning Assignment.

   An appropriate number of channel controls becomes active in the Surround Panner.

The Surround Panner

The Multichannel Encoder window contains the Surround Panner (**Figure 9.6**), which is a graphic representation of the surround-sound field and the perceived location of each track in relation to the listener (whose location is always at the center of the crosshairs). With a track selected in the Track List pane, you can move the panner point (the white dot) in the Surround Panner to any location to determine where the listener will think that sound is located (**Figure 9.7**).

If you place the panner point directly on top of one of the five channels or the subwoofer (marked LFE), the selected track will come only from that particular channel. If you place it anywhere else, the track will be sent to a particular combination of channels that will produce the appropriate effect.

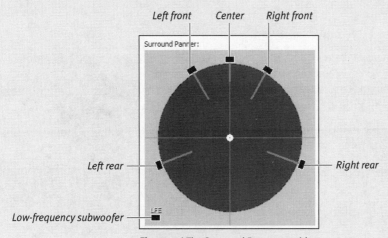

Figure 9.6 The Surround Panner provides a graphic representation of the surround-sound field and its six channels.

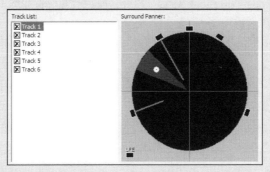

Figure 9.7 The location of the panner point (the white dot) in the Surround Panner represents the selected track's virtual location in relation to the listener.

Using Pan Envelopes

Pan envelopes enable you to change the panning of a track over time using the waveform display in the Multichannel Encoder window (**Figure 9.8**).

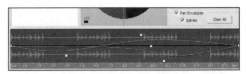

Figure 9.8 When you enable pan envelopes, two lines appear in the waveform display to help you change a track's panning over time.

To change a track's panning over time using pan envelopes:

1. Select a track in the Track List pane.

2. Choose either Surround Panner, Stereo source or Surround Panner, Summed to Mono from the Panning Assignment drop-down menu.

3. Select the Pan Envelopes check box.

    Two envelope lines, one green and one yellow, appear in the waveform display. (You may see only the yellow one at first, as it sits on top of the green one.)

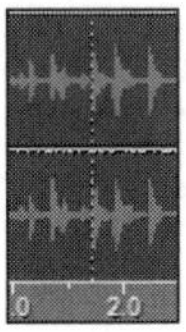

Figure 9.9 A vertical line in the waveform display indicates the place in your track where you want to adjust panning.

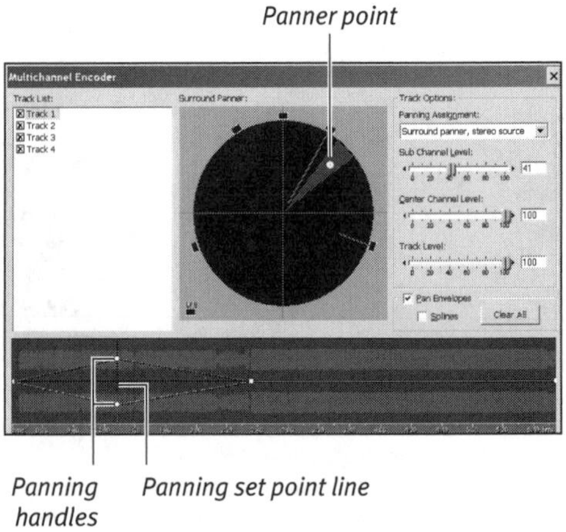

4. Check the Splines box if you want smoother panning transitions.

5. Click the waveform at a point for which you want to set panning.

    A vertical line appears in the waveform (**Figure 9.9**).

6. Set panning by dragging the panner point in the Surround Panner to the location you want.

    A pair of handles appears on the vertical line in the waveform (**Figure 9.10**). These handles move as you drag the panner point around the Surround Panner (and vice versa).

Figure 9.10 When you drag the panner point to a new location, a pair of handles for envelope adjustment appears in the waveform.

Figure 9.11 The Clear All button removes all Pan Envelope handles.

7. When you're through creating your panner point placements, drag the vertical playback cursor to the beginning of the waveform and click Play Track or Play All.

Watch the Surround Panner display change during playback to reflect your pan envelopes.

✔ Tips

■ You can create as many handles as you want on a pan envelope line in the waveform simply by clicking the line.

■ To delete a handle, drag it above or below the waveform display.

■ To remove all handles and return the pan envelopes to the default setting, click the Clear All button (**Figure 9.11**).

USING PAN ENVELOPES

Controlling Volume Levels

The Multichannel Encoder window contains three sliders for adjusting volume (**Figure 9.12**). You manipulate each one by moving it to the right to increase volume and to the left to decrease volume for the selected channel or track. As you adjust volume, the length of the light blue lines that extend from each channel in the Surround Panner display change to reflect your settings.

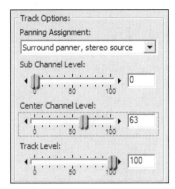

Figure 9.12 The Track Options pane contains three volume-adjustment sliders.

◆ **Sub Channel Level slider:** Specifies an amplitude for reproduction of the selected track in the subwoofer channel, regardless of where the track is panned in the surround-sound field. If this slider is set to 0, the track will not be sent to the subwoofer at all; if the track is panned to the subwoofer channel only, this slider acts as a straightforward volume control.

◆ **Center Channel Level slider:** Specifies how loud the center channel should be in relation to the front left and right channels.

◆ **Track Level slider:** Controls the volume of the selected track in the surround-sound field, regardless of its location or the selected surround-panning mode.

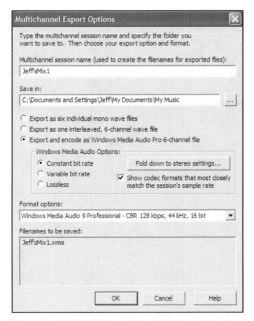

Figure 9.13 The Multichannel Export Options dialog box.

Saving Multichannel Audio

When you've tweaked, panned, and set up envelopes for all your tracks and channels and you're satisfied with your multichannel mix, it's time to save your work and export it to a file. You have several choices for exporting audio in the Multichannel Export Options dialog box.

To export multichannel audio to a file:

1. Click the Export button on the right side of the Multichannel Encoder window, under the waveform display.

   The Multichannel Export Options dialog box appears (**Figure 9.13**).

2. In the Multichannel Session Name field, enter a name you'd like Audition to use for any files that are generated.

3. In the Save In field, specify a folder where you want your files saved.

4. *Set export options to one of the following:*

   ▲ **Export as Six Individual Mono Wave Files:** Saves your six surround-sound channels as individual files in WAV format.

   ▲ **Export as One Interleaved, 6-Channel Wave File:** Saves your surround-sound mix in a single file in a WAV format that can be used with Dolby Digital encoders.

   ▲ **Export and Encode as Windows Media Audio Pro 6-Channel File:** Saves your surround-sound mix to a WMA file that can be played back on a multichannel-enabled Windows XP computer running Windows Media Player 9 or later.

   continues on next page

SAVING MULTICHANNEL AUDIO

5. Set other options in the windows and fields below (these will differ according to your selected export format; see the sidebar "A Few Notes on Formats and Compression").

6. Click OK.

Your multichannel-audio masterpiece is saved.

A Few Notes on Formats and Compression

When it comes time to export your multichannel audio, you have several format options, among them a vast array of compression choices for Windows Media Audio.

Unlike standard CD-Audio, which is uncompressed, Windows Media uses a compression algorithm to lower the bit rate of the audio stream (the number of bits of information per second of audio). Windows Media can produce audio quality equal to or better than LPCM (the CD standard) at lower bit rates and thus smaller file sizes. This can be very important if you're squeezing multichannel audio into a video project with a limited bit budget.

The Windows Media encoder in Audition uses two compression methods: constant bit rate (CBR) and variable bit rate (VBR). CBR is the faster, simpler approach: choose a bit rate (say, 128 Kbps), and the encoder will stick to it the whole way through.

VBR is more complicated: the encoder analyzes the audio to see how efficiently each segment can be compressed (for instance, by checking for redundancies and for sounds outside of the human ear's audible range) and determines the lowest possible bit rate for the desired quality. Less easily compressed segments are encoded at higher rates. Because VBR takes a more careful measure of the audio stream to be compressed, it can use a lower average bit rate than CBR and achieve equivalent results.

Under Format Options in the Export Options dialog box of the Multichannel Encoder, you'll notice that the encoding selections identified as most similar to your project's sample rate are lower for VBR than CBR. If you're creating a multichannel soundtrack for a video project and looking for a way to save some bits, exporting your multichannel audio to Windows Media VBR may be just what you need.

Mastering and Burning CDs | 10

Integrated CD-burning capability is new to Audition in version 1.5. Once you've prepared your files, you can simply move them to a CD track list in CD Project view and start creating your CD.

You'll most likely have already done plenty of editing of your files by the time you're ready to burn a CD, using tools we've discussed in previous chapters such as frequency analysis, equalization, compression, and other effects.

Sequencing and recording a CD can be the final step in the mastering process, but you may also want to make reference CDs periodically throughout a project so that you can pass them around for review or listen to them away from your PC.

In this chapter, I'll explain how to import tracks into CD Project view, normalize them so that they match each other in amplitude, set a variety of properties, and burn them to CD.

Creating a CD

To burn a CD, you need to bring your tracks into CD Project view. There, you can put them in the order you want and remove those that you don't want to use. The process is slightly different in Edit view and Multitrack view.

To add a track to a CD in Edit view:

1. Select the part of the waveform that you want to include on your CD, or leave the whole file unselected to use it in its entirety.

2. Choose Edit > Insert in CD Project or press Alt+Insert (**Figure 10.1**).

   Audition adds the file or selection after the last track in your CD project.

To add a track to a CD in Multitrack view:

1. Choose Edit > Mix Down to CD Project (**Figure 10.2**).

2. *Do one of the following:*

   ▲ To add all the tracks in a multitrack project, choose All Audio Clips.

   ▲ To choose just those tracks that are currently selected, choose Selected Audio Clips.

3. If you haven't saved the current session, the Save Session dialog appears. Click Yes to save your session.

   Audition mixes down the tracks and places a file called Mixdown in your CD project.

Figure 10.1 If a waveform is open in Edit view, you can choose Edit > Insert in CD Project to bring it into CD Project view.

Figure 10.2 If a session is open in Multitrack view, you can choose Edit > Mix Down to CD Project to bring it into CD Project view.

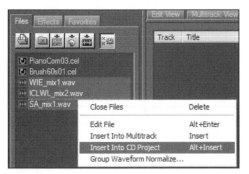

Figure 10.3 In the Organizer window, you can right-click selected tracks and select Insert into CD Project to bring them into CD Project view.

Insert into CD Project

Figure 10.4 The Insert into CD Project toolbar button.

Figure 10.5 The Insert file menu offers several options for inserting audio into CD Project view.

To add a track to a CD in the Organizer pane:

1. Select the track or tracks that you want to insert.

2. *Do one of the following:*

   ▲ Right-click the selected tracks and from the pop-up menu choose Insert into CD Project (**Figure 10.3**).

   ▲ Click the Insert into CD Project button (**Figure 10.4**).

   Audition adds the selected tracks to your CD project.

To add a track to a CD in CD Project view:

◆ *Do one of the following:*

   ▲ In the Organizer pane, select the track or tracks that you want to insert and drag them into the Display window.

   ▲ In the CD Project view, choose Insert > Audio, Insert > Audio from Video, or Insert > File/Cue List (**Figure 10.5**); then browse to the audio file you want and click Open.

   Any open files listed in the Organizer window's Files tab will also be offered as selections in this menu.

   ▲ Drag any supported audio file from your desktop or any Windows folder into the Display window in CD Project view.

CREATING A CD

155

To rearrange tracks in CD Project view:

1. Select the track or tracks that you want to move.

2. Click the Move Up or Move Down button to change the selected tracks' position in the lineup (**Figure 10.6**).

To remove tracks from CD Project view:

1. Select the track or tracks that you want to remove.

2. *Do one of the following:*
   ▲ Click the Remove button.
   ▲ Choose Edit > Remove Selected Tracks.

✔ Tips

■ You can click the Remove All button to clear the track list completely. You needn't select the tracks first.

■ If you decide you need to do some last-minute editing to a track in the CD Project view, right-click the track in the Display window and choose Edit File, or select the track and choose Edit > Waveform. Audition will open the file in Edit view.

■ Removing a track from the CD Project track list still leaves the related file available in Audition; it remains visible in the Organizer window. If you want to remove and close a track simultaneously, choose Edit > Destroy Selected Tracks (Remove and Close).

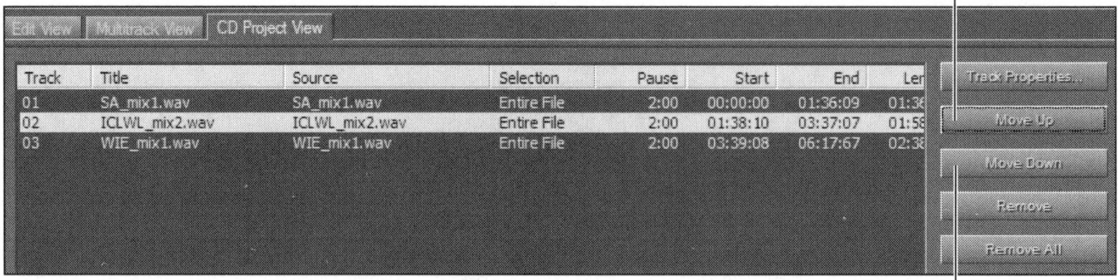

Move Up button

Move Down button

Figure 10.6 The Move Up and Move Down buttons in CD Project view allow you to tweak a CD track list.

CREATING A CD

Setting Track Properties

Once you've added a track in the CD Project view, you can set display properties for it, such as artist and song names. If your CD burner and player support CD-Text, the player will display this information as you listen to the disc.

Additional track properties settings include the following:

◆ **Pause:** Specifies the length of the pause between the preceding track and the current one on the CD.

◆ **Copy Protection:** If checked, sets the copy-protection flag to On. This prevents copying only on equipment that recognizes the copy-protection flag like the stereo-component "home" CD recorders.

◆ **Pre-Emphasis:** If checked, sets the pre-emphasis flag to On. This enables CD-player-based noise reduction on equipment that supports it.

◆ **ISRC:** Allows you to set an International Standard Recording Code (ISRC) number, which records country and year of origin, in addition to unique registrant and designation codes for commercially distributed CDs.

To set track properties:

1. Select a track in the CD Project view.

2. *Do one of the following*:
   ▲ Click the Track Properties button.
   ▲ Choose View > Track Properties.
   The Track Properties window opens
   (**Figure 10.7**).

3. Enter the track title and artist names in the appropriate fields.

4. Accept the default track property settings, or click the Use Custom Track Properties button to configure the settings you want to change.

5. Click OK.
   Track properties are now set.

✔ Tip

■ Select Same for All Tracks to apply the settings in the Track Properties pane to all tracks in a track list.

Figure 10.7 The Track Properties window.

Normalizing CD Tracks

One hallmark of a poorly mastered CD is inappropriate matching of volume levels. When a subdued, acoustic song sounds louder than the full-tilt rock number that preceded it, you know the mastering engineer didn't do a good job.

Audition includes the Group Waveform Normalize tool to help you control the relative volume of CD tracks so that they add up to a cohesive listening experience. During normalization, the program finds the loudest part of each waveform and then adjusts the waveforms' levels so that they all peak at the same amplitude. If the levels are raised, you can apply hard limiting during the process to avoid clipping (see "Effects Menu Options" in Chapter 6).

Settings in the Normalization pane include the following:

- **Normalization:** You can choose between normalizing to an average level (which the program determined during analysis on the Analyze Loudness tab) or to a particular dB level.

- **Use Equal Loudness Contour:** Checking this box helps ensure that all tracks are set to the same perceived amplitude.

- **Out of Band Peaks:** You can specify whether you want to use hard limiting to avoid clipping.

- **Statistics RMS Width:** This setting determines the length of an audio selection that Audition uses to determine Root-Mean-Square (RMS) values.

To normalize tracks in CD Project view:

1. Select Edit > Group Waveform Normalize.

   The Choose Files tab of the Group Waveform Normalize window opens (**Figure 10.8**).

2. Select the track or tracks that you want to normalize.

3. Display the Analyze Loudness tab (**Figure 10.9**).

4. Click the Scan for Statistical Information button.

   Audition analyzes tracks and displays amplitude information for each.

5. Display the Normalize tab (**Figure 10.10**).

6. Configure the settings.

7. Click Run Normalize.

   Audition adjusts the amplitude of each waveform according to your specifications.

✔ Tips

- The human ear can be fooled into perceiving volume disparities if amplitude peaks occur at the same decibel level but at different frequencies. The Use Equal Loudness Contour setting is designed to help make up for this.

- An RMS value tells you the average amplitude of an audio clip, and can be a better indication of perceived volume than a peak amplitude value.

Figure 10.8 On the Choose Files tab of the Group Waveform Normalize window, you can select the tracks you want to include in the normalization process.

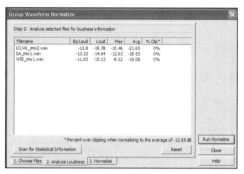

Figure 10.9 The Analyze Loudness tab of the Group Waveform Normalize window contains a powerful tool for analyzing the amplitude of audio files.

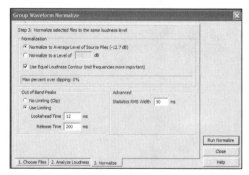

Figure 10.10 You complete the normalization process on the Normalize tab of the Group Waveform Normalize window.

Using the Analyze Loudness Tab

The Analyze Loudness tab provides valuable information about your waveforms. When you click the Scan for Statistical Information button, information appears for each waveform in the following fields:

♦ **Eq-Loud:** Specifies how much Audition will raise the amplitude of a file during normalization, if the Use Equal Loudness Contour is used (in the Normalize tab).

♦ **Loud:** Specifies how much Audition will raise the amplitude of a file during normalization if the Use Equal Loudness Contour is not used.

♦ **Max:** Displays the maximum RMS value that was found in the file.

♦ **Avg:** Displays the average RMS for the file.

♦ **% Clip:** Shows how much of the file would be clipped if the file were normalized without limiting.

♦ **Reset:** Clears all analysis statistics.

You can access more statistics for any track by double-clicking it on the Analyze Loudness tab. An Advanced Statistical Report window opens (**Figure 10.11**), which displays two graphs. The larger graph represents RMS levels for the track, and the smaller one displays a projected clipping profile.

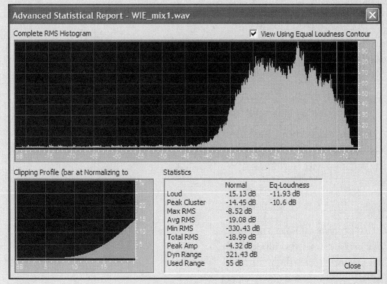

Figure 10.11 The Advanced Statistical Report window shows graphic representations of a file's amplitude and clipping levels.

NORMALIZING CD TRACKS

Burning a CD

Once you've created your CD track list and tweaked normalization settings and track properties, you can burn your CD within Audition.

To set up a CD recorder:

1. Choose Options > CD Device Properties.

   The CD Device Properties window opens (**Figure 10.12**).

2. In the Device menu, select the recordable drive you want to use.

3. Choose a buffer size and write speed.

4. Select the Buffer Underrun Prevention box if your recorder supports that feature.

5. Click OK.

   Your recorder is configured.

To write a CD:

1. Place a blank CD into your recorder.

2. Click the Write CD button (**Figure 10.13**), or choose File > Write CD.

   The Write CD window opens (**Figure 10.14**).

3. In the Write Mode drop-down menu, choose Test, Write, or Test & Write.

   The Test procedure determines whether your burner can handle your project with the current settings without buffer underruns.

4. If desired, select Eject CD When Complete.

5. If you want to include CD-Text information such as artist name and album title or a UPC/EAN code (a 13-digit number used to identify commercial CDs), select Write CD-Text.

6. Click Write CD.

   Disc writing begins. The Track and Disc bars indicate burning progress.

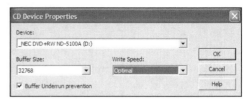

Figure 10.12 The CD Device Properties window.

Figure 10.13 The Write CD button in CD Project view.

Figure 10.14 The Write CD window.

AUDIO RESTORATION

Many of us enjoy hearing old recordings. Old records that meant something to us at a particular moment in time can bring back specific memories quite powerfully, and even our own old cassette tapes may hold priceless audio treasures that deserve archiving in a more secure format.

Bringing audio from old records, tapes, and other imperfect sources into Audition can be the first step in a superb restoration and archiving job. In this chapter, I'll introduce the tools in Audition that can help remove clicks and pops from old vinyl records, reduce hiss or other background noise in old tape recordings, and get rid of distortion, or clipping, in digital audio. Using these features will enable you to enjoy your precious audio keepsakes for a long time to come.

Eliminating Clicks and Pops

These days, more and more audiophiles (and other music fans who have never discarded, sold, or given away their record collections) are rediscovering the unique experience of listening to vinyl. Dance and hip-hop DJs and indie-rock fans have also contributed to the revival of interest in records and turntables.

There's no denying the tactile thrill of setting the needle down in a record's groove and enjoying music played on a high-quality phonograph. Nevertheless, one irrefutable fact about records is that they do not last forever, so many vinyl fans have adopted the practice of archiving their precious records onto CD-R or other digital media. Audition not only offers the ability to record audio to your hard drive from a phono preamp via a computer sound card (see Chapter 3), it can also remove the clicks and pops that can mar the sound of even the newest, cleanest records. The Noise Reduction submenu in the Effects menu contains two tools for eliminating clicks and pops: the Auto Click/Pop Eliminator tool and the Click/Pop Eliminator tool.

To use the Auto Click/Pop Eliminator tool:

1. *Do one of the following:*
   - ▲ Open your audio file and select a portion of the waveform from which you want to remove clicks and pops.
   - ▲ Choose Edit > Select Entire Wave to select all the audio.

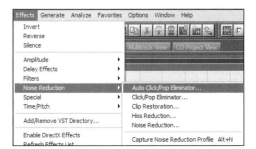

Figure 11.1 You'll find the Auto Click/Pop Eliminator and other restoration tools on the Noise Reduction submenu of the Effects menu.

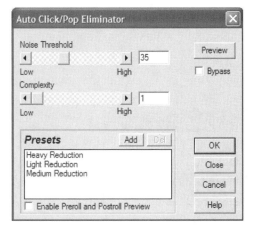

Figure 11.2 The Auto Click/Pop Eliminator window enables quick and easy automated removal of clicks and pops.

2. *Do one of the following:*
   ▲ Choose Effects > Noise Reduction > Auto Click/Pop Eliminator (**Figure 11.1**).
   ▲ Click the Effects tab in the Organizer window, expand Noise Reduction, and double-click Auto Click/Pop Eliminator.
   The Auto Click/Pop Eliminator window opens (**Figure 11.2**).

3. *Do one of the following:*
   ▲ Choose a Noise Threshold setting and then a Complexity setting.
   ▲ Select one of the three Click/Pop Reduction presets.

4. If you wish, click the Preview button to hear how your audio will sound with the settings you've chosen.

5. Click OK.
   The window closes, and your settings are applied.

✔ Tips

■ When choosing a Noise Threshold setting, keep in mind that lower settings remove more clicks and pops, but you may find that some essential elements of the audio track (such as music at certain frequencies) are removed as well. The default setting is 35; you can specify a setting between 1 and 100.

■ The higher the Complexity setting, the more your audio will be processed, which can degrade sound quality. The default setting is 1; you can specify a setting between 1 and 100.

■ As with other tools on the Effects menu, you can create presets for the effects in the Noise Reduction submenu to store your favorite settings for regular use. Three presets are available by default in the Auto Click/Pop Eliminator: Heavy, Light, and Medium reduction.

To use the Click/Pop Eliminator tool:

1. *Do one of the following:*

▲ Open your audio file and select a range from which you want to remove clicks and pops.

▲ Choose Edit > Select Entire Wave to select all the audio.

2. *Do one of the following:*

▲ Choose Effects > Noise Reduction > Click/Pop Eliminator.

▲ Click the Effects tab in the Organizer window, expand Noise Reduction, and double-click Click/Pop Eliminator.

The Click/Pop Eliminator window opens (**Figure 11.3**).

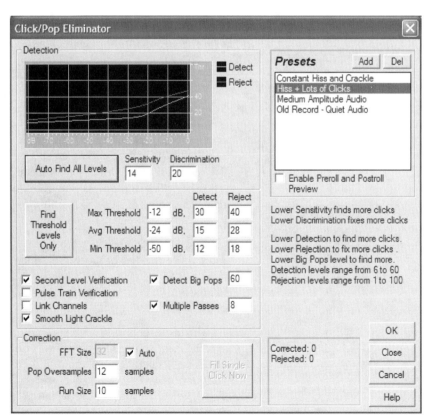

Figure 11.3
The Click/Pop Eliminator window allows more fine-tuning than its more automatic counterpart.

3. Configure the available settings, or select one of the four provided presets (or any additional presets that you have created).

4. If you wish, click the Preview button to hear how your audio will sound with the settings you've chosen.

5. Click OK.

The window closes, and your settings are applied.

✔ Tip

■ When configuring Click/Pop Eliminator settings, pay particular attention to the Detect thresholds, which determine sensitivity to clicks and pops (lower settings detect more), and the Reject thresholds, which determine how many potential clicks will be rejected and therefore not removed (lower settings remove more clicks).

Using Spectral View to Remove Clicks Manually

In Edit view's Spectral view, you can easily zero in on specific clicks or noises that you want to eliminate manually. Here's how:

◆ Choose View > Spectral View to switch from Waveform view to Spectral view.

◆ Choose Options > Settings.

◆ Open the Display tab (**Figure 11.4**).

◆ Adjust the Resolution and Window Width settings. This is analogous to zooming, and the Audition documentation recommends a Resolution setting of 256 bands and a Window Width setting of 40 percent for this type of editing.

◆ Click OK.

◆ In the Spectral view display, look for the clicks you want to remove. They will appear as vertical lines spanning the height of the display.

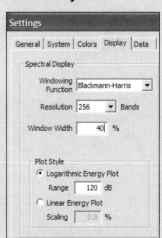

Figure 11.4 To zero in on specific clicks or pops in a file, you can manually adjust the view options for the Spectral view on the Settings window's Display tab.

Tips for Making Vinyl Transfers

The practice of transferring vinyl records to a digital format such as CD-R (known among aficionados as making "needle drops") has become popular as more and more people have grown interested in archiving their vinyl treasures. Here are some tips on how to get the best results when making a needle drop:

◆ Invest in some good cleaning products for both your records and your stylus and learn to use them properly and regularly—particularly if you like to pick up used vinyl at flea markets and thrift shops. Why rely on Audition to remove clicks and pops caused by dust and other debris when they can be removed at the source?

◆ Check the setup and alignment of your turntable, tonearm, and cartridge regularly to coax the best possible sound from (and prevent damage to) your precious vinyl. Examine the stylus for wear; a worn or damaged cartridge should be replaced.

◆ If your turntable is connected to a standalone phono preamplifier (or "phono stage"), run the outputs of that preamp directly into your sound card, preferably via the Line In jack (as opposed to the microphone, which provides a more boxy sound). If you use a preamp in a receiver or integrated amplifier, you can use its tape or preamp-out outputs. Never try to connect a turntable directly to your sound card; a phono preamp is always needed for a phono signal.

◆ For best results when transferring mono records, sum the stereo signal coming from your phono preamp to mono, either by using a Y-adapter wire or by recording to a mono waveform in Audition. This will provide a more solid center-channel mono sound and can help reduce the amount of background and surface noise.

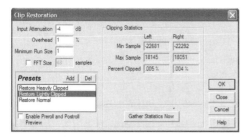

Figure 11.5 In the Clip Restoration window, you can configure settings to help get rid of digital distortion, or clipping.

Using Clip Restoration

Many of us who used to make mix tapes with our cassette recorders learned the dangers of setting recording levels too high. The resulting recording sounded fuzzy, distorted, and generally unpleasant. In addition, when recording levels are set too high in a digital recording, the resulting distortion can sound like high-pitched squealing, loud popping, or an unpleasant overlay of static.

Digital distortion, or clipping, results when the amplitude of a recorded signal is higher than the selected bit rate can handle. If you have an audio file that's marred by clipping, and re-recording is not an option, you can use Audition's Clip Restoration tool to replace the clipping sounds with new audio.

To use the Clip Restoration tool:

1. *Do one of the following:*
   ▲ Open your audio file and select a range from which you want to remove clipping.
   ▲ Choose Edit > Select Entire Wave to select all the audio.

2. *Do one of the following:*
   ▲ Choose Effects > Noise Reduction > Clip Restoration.
   ▲ Click the Effects tab in the Organizer window, expand Noise Reduction, and double-click Clip Restoration.

   The Clip Restoration window opens (**Figure 11.5**).

3. Configure the available settings.

4. If you wish, click the Preview button to hear how your audio will sound with the settings you've chosen.

5. Click OK.
   The window closes, and your settings are applied.

Reducing Noise and Hiss

The noise- and hiss-reduction tools in Audition perform similar tasks: they remove unwanted noise from your audio. Examples of such noise include tape hiss (from cassettes or any other tape source), turntable-motor rumble, hum, microphone noise, amplifier buzzing, and any other extraneous noise that gets in the way of clean, clear audio.

The primary difference between the Noise Reduction and Hiss Reduction tools is that the former can reduce broadband background noise that extends across a wide frequency range, while the latter targets noise that falls below a particular amplitude threshold (called the noise floor), leaving other frequencies unaffected.

To use the Noise Reduction tool:

1. Open your audio file and select a range at least a half-second in length that contains the noise you want to reduce.

2. *Do one of the following:*
   ▲ Choose Effects > Noise Reduction > Capture Noise Reduction Profile.
   ▲ Click the Effects tab in the Organizer window, expand Noise Reduction, and double-click Capture Noise Reduction Profile.

3. Select a range in the waveform in which you want to reduce the noise captured in step 2.

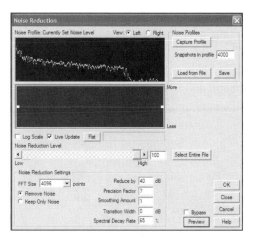

Figure 11.6 The Noise Reduction window enables you to remove background noise across a wide frequency spectrum.

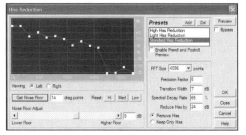

Figure 11.7 The Hiss Reduction window allows you to reduce tape hiss and other noise that exists below a specific noise floor.

4. *Do one of the following:*

▲ Choose Effects > Noise Reduction > Noise Reduction.

▲ Click the Effects tab in the Organizer window, expand Noise Reduction, and double-click Noise Reduction.

The Noise Reduction window opens (**Figure 11.6**).

5. Configure the available settings.

6. If you wish, click the Preview button to hear how your audio will sound with the settings you've chosen.

7. Click OK.

The window closes, and your settings are applied.

✔ Tip

■ If possible, your selected range for noise reduction should include *only* the noise and no music; try a snippet at the very beginning or very end of the waveform.

To use the Hiss Reduction tool:

1. *Do one of the following:*

▲ Open your audio file and select a range from which you want to reduce hiss.

▲ Choose Edit > Select Entire Wave to select all the audio.

2. *Do one of the following:*

▲ Choose Effects > Noise Reduction > Hiss Reduction.

▲ Click the Effects tab in the Organizer window, expand Noise Reduction, and double-click Hiss Reduction.

The Hiss Reduction window opens (**Figure 11.7**).

continues on next page

REDUCING NOISE AND HISS

3. Configure the available settings, or select one of the three provided presets (or any additional ones that you have created).

4. If you wish, click the Preview button to hear how your audio will sound with the settings you've chosen.

5. Click OK.

The window closes, and your settings are applied.

✔ Tip

■ When configuring Hiss Reduction settings, pay particular attention to the Get Noise Floor button, which analyzes your clip and estimates the noise floor (which you can fine-tune using the graph display) to help you remove hiss only, and not music.

REDUCING NOISE AND HISS

AUDITION FOR VIDEO PROJECTS

The integration of Audition into the Adobe Video Collection puts another powerful tool into the hands of video pros and hobbyists. Audition's ability to interact with and complement Adobe's Premiere Pro and After Effects video software helps make the Video Collection a versatile set of tools.

In this chapter, you'll learn how to embed a link in an exported audio file to the Audition session that it came from, so that the session can be reopened and tweaked when the file is used in Premiere Pro or After Effects. You'll also learn how to bring video clips into Audition itself and then edit the audio and preview its integration with the video.

Linking Exports to Sessions

Once you've created audio in Audition and exported it to a WAV file, you can import it into your video project in Adobe Premiere Pro or After Effects. But what if you then decide you need to make changes to the audio?

Thankfully, you can do this easily without manually reopening Audition and re-exporting your newly edited audio. The Adobe Video Collection offers round-tripping between several of the tools in the Video Collection, such as layered Photoshop documents exported to Encore DVD for DVD menu creation, which can be reopened in Photoshop, layers intact, for further editing. The same functionality is available for Audition. You can embed a link in your audio from the start that will enable you to call up Audition right from within Premiere Pro or After Effects via the Edit Original command and then edit your audio as you see fit.

To link exported audio to an Audition session:

1. In Audition, choose Options > Settings.

2. Open the Data tab (**Figure 12.1**).

3. Select the box next to Embed Project Link Data for Edit Original Functionality.

4. Click OK.

✔ Tip

■ Make sure, when you export your audio, that you select Save Extra Non-Audio Information in the File > Export > Audio dialog box (**Figure 12.2**). If you don't, the Edit Original command in the video software won't work.

Figure 12.1 Select Embed Project Link Data for Edit Original Functionality on the Data tab of the Options > Settings menu to enable editing of audio clips in Audition from within a video file in Premiere Pro or After Effects.

Figure 12.2 Select Save Extra Non-Audio Information in the File > Export > Audio dialog box to enable the Edit Original command when the file is imported into Premiere Pro or After Effects.

To edit audio in Audition from within Premiere Pro or After Effects:

1. In your Premiere Pro or After Effects video project, choose the audio file you want to edit.

2. Choose Edit > Edit Original (**Figure 12.3**). Audition opens, and the audio file is presented in either the Edit or Multitrack view, depending on where you exported it from (**Figure 12.4**).

3. Edit the audio or session in Audition.

4. *Do one of the following:*

   ▲ In Edit view, choose File > Save.

   ▲ In Multitrack view, choose File > Export > Audio and overwrite the original file.

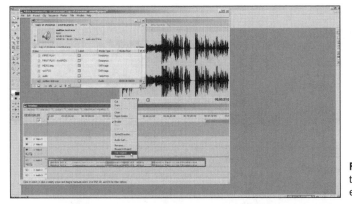

Figure 12.3 Choose Edit > Edit Original to tell Premiere Pro to open a file for editing in Audition.

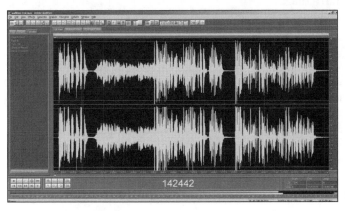

Figure 12.4 The file opens in Audition.

Importing Video Files

In the Multitrack view, you can import both the audio and video from a video file, though you should remember that you can use only one video clip at a time. This allows you to match the audio to the video exactly as you wish, with video thumbnails appearing in the track display. Note that you can't trim or otherwise edit the video in Audition.

To import audio from a video file:

◆ *Do one of the following:*

  ▲ In Edit view, choose File > Open Audio from Video (**Figure 12.5**).

  ▲ In Multitrack view, select a track, put the cursor at the point at which you want the audio to begin, and choose Insert > Audio from Video (**Figure 12.6**).

To import audio and video from a video file:

◆ In Multitrack view, select a track, put the cursor at the point at which you want the video to begin, and choose Insert > Video.

✔ Tips

■ You can see more or fewer thumbnails in the track display by zooming in or out.

■ When you bring a video clip into a track in Multitrack view, the corresponding audio is dropped into the track beneath it (**Figure 12.7**). Because the audio and video occupy different tracks, you can move them separately. Depending on the situation, this may or may not be desirable; to prevent the audio and video from being moved out of sync, create a clip group containing both the audio and video (see Chapter 8 for information on creating clip groups).

Figure 12.5 The File > Open Audio from Video command brings audio from a video clip into Audition's Edit view.

Figure 12.6 The Insert > Audio from Video command brings audio from a video clip into Audition's Multitrack view.

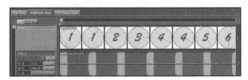

Figure 12.7 When a video clip is brought into Multitrack view, the video is dropped into one track, and the corresponding audio is dropped into the track beneath the video.

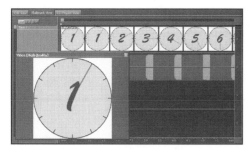

Figure 12.8 You can preview your video clip in Multitrack view's Video window.

Hide/Show Video Window

Figure 12.9
The Hide/Show Video Window button in the Multitrack view's toolbar.

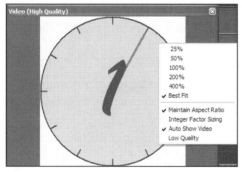

Figure 12.10 Right-click the Video window to configure its settings.

Previewing Video

The dockable Video window (**Figure 12.8**) enables you to watch your video during playback at a larger size than the track display can offer. You can show (or hide) the Video window by clicking the Hide/Show Video Window button on the toolbar (**Figure 12.9**).

The Video window comes with its own set of configurable options.

To configure Video window settings:

1. Right-click the Video window.

   A pop-up menu opens (**Figure 12.10**).

2. *Do any of the following:*

   ▲ To set a specific window size, select a zoom percentage, or choose Best Fit to enable an automatic setting.

   ▲ To prevent the image from widening or otherwise losing its proper horizontal-to-vertical ratio when you resize it, select Maintain Aspect Ratio.

   ▲ To restrict preview resizing to simple, integer-based ratios, which avoids resampling and generally provides better performance, select Integer Factor Sizing.

   ▲ To display the Video window by default when you import a video clip, select Auto Show Video.

   ▲ To decrease the quality of the preview (if, for example, you want to save system resources), select Low Quality.

✔ Tip

■ A change in the preview quality setting will not take effect until the video clip is reimported into Audition.

PREVIEWING VIDEO

Adding Narration to Video

The ability to edit audio tracks in Audition can be invaluable to a Premiere Pro editor's efforts. For instance, Audition can be used to punch up soundtrack quality, create a two-channel mix where only a single channel was before, or apply sophisticated audio restoration tools to clean up extraneous noise captured in an on-site video shoot under less than optimum conditions (see Chapter 11).

Audition can also assist in a video project when you're creating a narration track. Let's say you're piecing together a documentary, and you're assembling all the elements in the editing room. You have establishing shots, live event footage, and a range of archival material, both video and still images. And like documentarian extraordinaire Ken Burns, you've added motion to your photographs, deliberate pans and zooms to specific elements of photographs to highlight, say, key individuals in a crowd.

You have lots of great footage, you've spent weeks poring over the video edits in Premiere. What's more, you've carefully scripted your voice narration to hit all the right points at all the right times. But it's virtually impossible to pace your narration to hit all these points on cue—and all your work is for naught without pinpoint synchronization with the narration track.

Enter Audition, with its ability to time-stretch and compress audio clips without affecting pitch (see "Using Clips" in Chapter 8). This feature can save you innumerable takes with the voice talent and salvage virtually any project, from a full-length documentary to a 30-second ad spot.

Audition also gives you the ability to preview audio and video simultaneously. Then you can send your edited project file back and forth between Audition and Premiere until you get it right, project parameters intact.

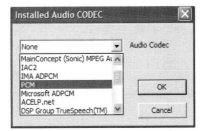

Figure 12.11 When exporting a video clip, you can choose from a variety of audio-compression codecs.

Exporting Video Files

When your audio is just the way you want it and is matched correctly with the video in your clip, you're ready to export it back to a video file.

To export to a video file:

1. Choose File > Export > Video.
   The Export Video dialog box opens.

2. Browse to the folder where you want to save your file.

3. Enter a name for your file.

4. Optionally, click the Options button to choose an audio-compression codec (**Figure 12.11**).

5. Make sure the Save Extra Non-Audio Information check box is selected.

6. Click OK.
   The file is saved with its new Audition-tweaked soundtrack.

7. Reopen the file in Premiere Pro or After Effects as desired and continue your video editing.

INDEX

INDEX

INDEX